The Yellowstone National Park

THE

Yellowstone

NATIONAL

PARK

☆ ☆ ☆ ☆ ☆ ☆ ☆ ☆ ☆ ☆ ☆

HIRAM MARTIN CHITTENDEN

EDITED AND WITH AN INTRODUCTION
BY RICHARD A. BARTLETT

Norman
University of Oklahoma Press

By Richard A. Bartlett

Great Surveys of the American West (Norman, 1962)
The Yellowstone National Park, by Hiram Martin Chittenden (ed.) (Norman, 1964)
A Trip to the Yellowstone National Park in July, August, and September, 1875, by General W. E. Strong (ed.) (Norman, 1968)

Library of Congress Catalog Card Number: 64-11334

New edition copyright © 1964 by the University of Oklahoma Press, Norman, Publishing Division of the University. Manufactured in the U.S.A. First printing, 1964; second printing, 1964; third printing, 1967; fourth printing, 1971; fifth printing, 1973; sixth printing, 1976; seventh printing, 1977; eighth printing, 1979; ninth printing, 1982.

EDITOR'S INTRODUCTION

NOT MANY of today's visitors to the Park make use of the North Entrance. This route, southward out of Gardiner, Montana, is the most remote from our centers of population, and save for the Mammoth Hot Springs, it is farther than are the other gateways from the Park's main attractions. But before the day of the pickup truck camper and the house trailer, this entrance was the most accessible. Sightseers rode the Northern Pacific to Cinnabar Station or Gardiner, and then transferred to the open-air, bright yellow, horse-drawn coaches of the transportation company which held the franchise. When all the passengers were seated the coachman yelled giddap and the tourist-filled tallyho clattered over the graveled road into the Yellowstone for a five-day tour of the land of wonders.

After 1903, as they crossed the Park boundary, tourists passed through a great stone entrance called the Roosevelt Memorial Arch. This impressive monument is still there today, and those few who still enter from Gardiner may read its inscriptions: For the Benefit and Enjoyment of the People: Yellowstone National Park: Created by Act of Congress: March 1, 1872.

March 1, 1872. That is sixty-nine years after the purchase of Louisiana and the beginning of Lewis and Clark's remarkable expedition; it is twenty-six years after the annexation of Oregon, twenty-four years after the end of the Mexican War and the acquisition of California and the Southwest, twenty-three years after the California gold rush, thirteen years after the Pike's Peak rush, seven years after the Civil War, and three years after the completion of the transcontinental railroad. It is a little more than three years before the Custer massacre and five years before Chief Joseph and the Nez Percés went on the warpath.

"Created by Act of Congress: March 1, 1872." That places its passage in the days of President Grant. This is in the midst of the Robber Baron era, the era of the "Great Barbecue," when money could buy anything in Washington and the public domain was being ruthlessly despoiled. This was an era of business titans and of political mediocrities. There were land grabs and salary grabs, gold corners and whisky frauds. But as for "the people"—who ever considered them? Yet here is the Yellowstone National Park, established "for the benefit and enjoyment of the people," in 1872. How did this come about, and who was responsible for it? In the answers lie many interesting stories.

Even though someone was able to save this land of miracles for the people, how was the Act of 1872 administered? For passage of an act is only a first step, its success depending upon the vigor with which the act is administered. In the milieu of the 1870's, 1880's, and 1890's, how were private interests prevented from using politics to exploit an area whose wonders aroused the curiosity of millions, among whom were many thousands willing to part with substantial change in order to view the geysers, hot springs, falls, and the Grand Canyon of the Yellowstone in person. How were poachers dealt with? Who gained the concessions? Who planned the road system? Who were the sentries, official and unofficial, who protected the Yellowstone "for the people" until the time when the government would have a clear concept of the national park idea, and could be trusted to administer and preserve the Park—and others which would follow—with the tender loving care which such areas deserve?

There were many sentries in those formative years, casting suspicious eyes upon every effort made by selfish men to hack away at the Yellowstone Park bastion. Surely in the vanguard of these self-appointed defenders was Captain (eventually Brigadier General) Hiram Martin Chittenden, of the U.S. Army Corps of Engineers. Many of his assignments took him west and his love of the land of limitless space soon passed beyond the more popular realm of dream idolatry into the arena of solid historical research. In due time Captain Chittenden, trained as a civil engineer, emerged as a competent historian with a clear, spritely style. For one man to be a good army officer, a top-drawer engineer, and a competent historian concurrently is an unusual phenomenon, and indeed, Hiram Martin Chittenden was a man of unusual and considerable talents.

He was born October 25, 1858, and spent his boyhood close to Yorkshire, New York, in a beautiful region about halfway between Lake Erie and the Finger Lakes. After a so-so public school education he entered West Point, graduating third in a class of thirty-seven in 1884. Assigned to the Corps of Engineers, he worked on various projects, first coming to the Yellowstone in 1891 after a two-year tour on the Missouri River above Sioux City. Although he was not yet fully recovered from a siege of typhoid fever, Chittenden pitched into road planning and building with enthusiasm. During the span of his two tours of duty in the Park (1891–93, 1899–1906), he supervised some four hundred miles of road construction. Such projects as the Roosevelt Memorial Arch at Gardiner, the arch bridge over the Yellowstone above the Upper Falls (since replaced but appropriately named the Chittenden Memorial Bridge), and the road up Mount Washburn attest to his engineering skill.

Yet these physical manifestations of his love of the West, and of the Yellowstone, did not suffice. The country cast a magic spell over him. "There was at the time the irresistable 'call of the wild,' " he later wrote, "grandeur of scenery, cerulean skies, the entrancing lure of the forest trails, and those myriad other inspiring influences which make one content to accept a mountain life as one's permanent lot. The spell was a real one. . . ."[1] For Chittenden, it was reflected in a deep and abiding ambition. Successful army officer and civil engineer that he was, he cherished the desire to write. Having abandoned the realm of fiction, he turned to western history, and the topic that loomed nearest to him was the Yellowstone. Realizing his amateur status, he consulted with Dr. Elliott Coues who, although an army surgeon, had already established a reputation as a historian. Then the young engineer pitched into his project with a vengeance. He wrote most of it following his first tour of duty in the Park, while stationed at Louisville, Kentucky, and Columbus, Ohio.[2] *The Yellowstone National Park: Historical and Descriptive,* was finally published in 1895.

Although he considered the work "somewhat amateurish and freakish," it was an immediate success, and has since run through many editions. Thus assured of his ability, Chittenden went on to become a prolific historian during the next ten years, publishing *The American Fur Trade of the Far West* in 1902, the *History of Early Steamboat Navigation on the Missouri: Life and Adventures of Joseph LaBarge,* in 1903, and, in collaboration with Alfred T. Richardson, the *Life, Letters, and Travels of Father Pierre-Jean De Smet, S.J.,* in 1904–1905. In the half-century and more which has passed since he published these works, much additional research has been accomplished; but the scope, clarity, and reasonably good research in Chittenden's books make them of continued value to historians.

Of all the subjects about which he wrote, none so interested the Captain as the early history of the Yellowstone National Park. This was a work of dedication as well as of history, for he was genuinely concerned about the future of the Park; and a readily available, authoritative and lucid history might ac-

[1] H. M. Chittenden, *The Yellowstone National Park: Historical and Descriptive* (Second general revision. Cincinnati, Stewart and Kidd, Co., 1915), iv.

[2] Bruce Leroy (ed.), *H. M. Chittenden: A Western Epic, Being a Selection from His Unpublished Journals, Diaries, and Reports* (Tacoma, Washington State Historical Society, 1961), 21.

complish substantial returns in increasing the number of its defenders. Furthermore, as he soon discovered, the history of the Yellowstone was a complex and fascinating blend of man and nature, of howling wilderness and rampant civilization.

He commenced his book by tracking down the source of the very name "Yellowstone," tracing it possibly to the explorations of the Sieur de la Verendrye in 1743 and the subsequent name used by the French trappers when Lewis and Clark wintered at the Mandan villages, *Roche Jaune*. Then he described the Indians who surrounded the Park—the Crows, Blackfeet, and Shoshones—and discussed the miserable few who actually lived in the Yellowstone, the *Tukarikas*, or Sheepeaters, who were a segment of the Shoshones. The Captain traced the Indian trails across the Park, and discussed the apparent lack of interest manifested by the Indians in the fabulous area.

Into the story came the first important white man, John Colter, frontiersman, explorer, trapper, very man among manly men, who appears to have explored the Yellowstone and its environs in 1807, only to be ridiculed for his fantastic stories when he spun them around frontiersmen's campfires. Subsequently into the story stepped that white barbarian, the fur trapper; and probably members of that grizzled fraternity witnessed the geysers, and perhaps once a trapper's rendezvous was actually held in Yellowstone's Hayden Valley. Then the beaver declined in number, peltry fell in value as beaver hats went out of style, and the heyday of the fur trade came to an end. And still, the Yellowstone was unknown to the public.

Gradually, however, rumors persisted until thoughtful men gave them a measure of credence. Chittenden traced a number of the early stories, and then devoted an entire chapter to that old liar (as everyone assumed the old frontiersman to be), Jim Bridger. By this time it was the 1850's, and toward the end of that decade the United States Army entered the picture, sending Captain W. F. Raynolds in 1859 toward the Yellowstone and on northward for an ideal study of an impending eclipse. But Raynolds did not break through the snow-filled mountain barriers, and then the Civil War intervened, and his report was set aside until hostilities ended. The discovery of gold, however, surmounted the obstacles of the Civil War, and when the Alder Gulch rush in present Montana got under way in 1863, the days of the Yellowstone secrets were numbered.

In a separate chapter Chittenden dealt with the final discovery of the Yellowstone, following the routes of the Folsom–Cook–Peterson party of 1869 and the Washburn–Langford–Doane expedition of 1870, as well as the Hayden survey of 1871 which gave scientific confirmation of the wonders of the Yellowstone. He also explained how the Yellowstone National Park came into being, giving the deserving men in the story their due credit for passage of the bill creating the Park "for all the people."

Completing Section I of his book, the historical narration, Chittenden discussed the reasons for Yellowstone's tardy discovery, the tragic march through the Park of Chief Joseph and the Nez Percés, and something about the early administration of the area. In a third section the Captain discussed questions involving the future of the Park. Section II, which was entirely descriptive, is now outdated and has been omitted from this edition. It is, then, the historical sections which are here republished. They remain sound and entertaining history, dealing in a complete fashion with the early story of the Yellowstone. They retain something of the charm of the years in which they were written. They are enjoyable reading.

No attempt has been made to change this first, 1895 edition into an up-to-date history of the Yellowstone. Such an approach would defeat the purposes of this book. It is and it remains the early history of the Yellowstone area to the year 1895. There are, of course, a few corrections of errors, and the footnotes have been changed as follows: All of Chittenden's citations, indicated by asterisks, have been changed into modern research style, with no changes whatsoever in the meaning. Footnotes presenting new information or additional clarification by the editor have been numbered—the editor's footnotes are the *only numbered* footnotes in the text. Finally, a short bibliography of materials available in most city libraries has been included, replacing the older listing which is quite useless.

All of the maps reproduced in this book, as is made clear in the list of maps on page xxi, are of historical interest only. Necessarily they have had to be greatly reduced in order to be accommodated in this volume, but those who wish to peruse them with a reading glass will find them all the more rewarding.

Even in a brief editing job such as this one, thanks are in order—to Dean John K. Folger and the Florida State University Research Council which provided means for me to do some work at Mammoth Hot Springs, and incidentally to ground myself physically in the Yellowstone terrain; to Mr. Archibald Hanna, curator of the Western Americana Collection at Yale, for aid in tracking down one of Chittenden's faulty citations; to Mr. John M. Good, the Park Naturalist and Executive Secretary of the Yellowstone Library and Museum Association, who first suggested this revision; and most especially to Mr. Aubrey L. Haines, the Yellowstone Park Historian, with whom I conversed at length and whose always excellent advice has been most appreciated. For any errors in the editing, I assume full responsibility.

And now it is approaching sundown, and the great sunbeams cast themselves sky-eastward from behind Electric Peak, and Captain Chittenden's Roosevelt Memorial Arch darkens with the twilight, but the inscription stands out: "For the Benefit and Enjoyment of the People."

Richard A. Bartlett

*Library of the Yellowstone Library
  and Museum Association*
Mammoth Hot Springs
Yellowstone National Park, Wyoming

To the memories of John Colter and James Bridger
Pioneers in the Wonderland of the Upper Yellowstone

AUTHOR'S PREFACE

TWENTY-FIVE YEARS AGO, this date, a company of gentlemen were encamped at the Forks of the Madison River in what is now the Yellowstone National Park. They had just finished the first complete tour of exploration ever made of that region. Fully realizing the importance of all they had seen, they asked what ought to be done to preserve so unique an assemblage of wonders to the uses for which Nature had evidently designed them. It required no argument to show that government protection alone was equal to the task, and it was agreed that a movement to secure such protection should be inaugurated at once. So rapidly did events develop along the line of this idea, that within the next eighteen months the "Act of Dedication" had become a law, and the Yellowstone National Park took its place in our country's history.

The widespread interest which the discovery of this region created among civilized peoples has in no degree diminished with the lapse of time. In this country particularly the Park to-day stands on a firmer basis than ever before. The events of the past two years, in matters of legislation and administration, have increased many fold the assurances of its continued preservation, and have shown that even the petty local hostility, which has now and then menaced its existence, is yielding to a wiser spirit of patriotism.[1]

The time therefore seems opportune, in passing so im-

1 Chittenden is referring to two acts passed by Congress in 1894: the "National Park Protective Act" and "An Act Concerning Leases in the Yellowstone National Park." *28 U.S. Statutes at Large*, 73–75, 222–23. See Appendix B.

portant an epoch in the history of the Park, and while many of the actors in its earlier scenes are still among us, to collect the essential facts, historical and descriptive, relating to this region, and to place them in form for permanent preservation. The present literature of the Park, although broad in scope and exhaustive in detail, is unfortunately widely scattered, somewhat difficult of access, and in matters of early history, notably deficient. To supply a work which shall form a complete and connected treatment of the subject, is the purpose of the present volume. . . .

In describing a region whose fame rests upon its natural wonders, the assistance of the illustrative art has naturally been resorted to. The various accompanying maps have all been prepared especially for this work and are intended to set forth not only present geography but historical features as well. The folded map embodies every thing to date from the latest geographical surveys. It will bear careful study, and this has been greatly simplified by a system of marginal references to be used with the list of names in Appendix A.[2]

The illustrations cover every variety of subject in the Park and represent the best results of photographic work in that region. They are mostly from the studio of Mr. F. J. Haynes, of St. Paul, the well-known Park photographer, who has done so much by his art to disseminate a knowledge of the wonders of the Yellowstone. A considerable number are from views taken during the Hayden surveys by Mr. William H. Jackson, now of Denver, Colorado. A few excellent subjects are from the amateur work of Captain C. M. Gandy, Assistant Surgeon, U.S.A., who was stationed for some years on duty in the Park. The portraits are restricted to the few early explorers who visited the Upper Yellowstone prior to the creation of the Park.[3]

To any one who is familiar with the recent history of the Park, a work like the present would seem incomplete without some reference to those influences which endanger its future

[2] This map has been reduced in size in the present edition and is on p. 145.

[3] New illustrations, some of them by Jackson, were gathered for the present edition, since the ones from the 1895 edition would not reproduce satisfactorily.

existence. A brief discussion of this subject is accordingly presented, which, without considering particular schemes, exposes the dangerous tendencies underlying them all.

In the course of a somewhat extended correspondence connected with the preparation of this work, the author has become indebted for much information that could not be found in the existing literature of the Park. He desires in this place to return his sincere acknowledgments to all who have assisted him, and to refer in a special manner:

To the Hon. N. P. Langford, of St. Paul, whose long acquaintance with the Upper Yellowstone country has made him an authority upon its history.

To Dr. Elliott Coues, of Washington, D.C., who has contributed, besides much general assistance, the essential facts relating to the name "Yellowstone."

To Captain George S. Anderson, Sixth U.S. Cavalry, Superintendent of the Park, for the use of his extensive collection of Park literature.

To Prof. Arnold Hague, and others, of the U.S. Geological Survey, for many important favors.

To Prof. J. D. Butler, of Madison, Wis., for biographical data relating to James Bridger.

To Dr. R. Ellsworth Call, of Cincinnati, Ohio, for valuable assistance pertaining to the entire work.

To the Hon. D. M. Browning, Commissioner of Indian Affairs, for important data relating to the Indian tribes in the vicinity of the Yellowstone Park.

To the officers of the War and Interior Department, the U.S. Fish Commission, the U.S. Bureau of Ethnology, and of the U.S. Coast and Geodetic Survey, for public documents and other information of great value.

To R. T. Durrett, LL.D., of Louisville, Ky.; Mr. J. G. Morrison, of the Library of Congress, Washington, D.C.; Mr. J. D. Losecamp, of Billings, Mont.; Mr. George Bird Grinnell, of *Forest and Stream,* New York City; Major James F. Gregory, Corps of Engineers, U.S.A.; Lieutenant Wm. H. Bean, Second Cavalry, U.SA.; Hon. David E. Folsom, White Sulphur Springs, Mont.; Washington Mathews, Major and Surgeon, U.S.A.; Dr. A.C. Peale, of Philadelphia, Pa.; William Hallett Phillips, of Washington, D.C.; Dr. Lyman B. Sperry, of Bellevue, O.; Mrs. Matilda Cope Stevenson, of Washington, D.C.; Mrs. Sirena J. Washburn, of Greencastle, Ind.; Miss Isabel Jelke, of Cincinnati, O.; Mr. O. B. Wheeler, of St. Louis, Mo.; Mr. O. D. Wheeler, of St. Paul, Minn.; Mr. J. H. Baronett, of Livingston, Mont.; Mr. W. T. Hamilton, of Columbus, Mont.; Mr. Richard Leigh, of Wilford, Idaho; Mr. Edwin L. Berthoud, of Golden, Colo.; and Miss Laura S. Brown, of Columbus, O.

H. M. C.

COLUMBUS, OHIO, *September 19, 1895.*

CONTENTS

ILLUSTRATIONS

Between pages 42–43
Hiram Martin Chittenden, Crow Warrior
Blackfoot Warriors, Tukuarika Shoshone
Bannock Family, John Colter's Race for Life
Jim Bridger, Chief Joseph

Between pages 106–107
Chief Looking Glass, Mammoth Hot Springs
Lower Falls of the Yellowstone, Old Faithful Geyser
George Catlin, General Henry Dana Washburn
Ferdinand Vandiveer Hayden, Nathaniel Pitt Langford

MAPS OF HISTORICAL INTEREST

The Yellowstone National Park

☆ 1 ☆

"YELLOWSTONE"

LEWIS AND CLARK passed the first winter of their famous trans-continental expedition among the Mandan Indians, on the Missouri River, sixty-six miles above the present capital of North Dakota. When about to resume their journey in the spring of 1805, they sent back to President Jefferson a report of progress and a map of the western country based upon information derived from the Indians. In this report and upon this map appear for the first time, in any official document, the words "Yellow Stone" as the name of the principal tributary of the Missouri.

It seems, however, that Lewis and Clark were not the first actually to use the name. David Thompson, the celebrated explorer and geographer, prominently identified with the British fur trade in the Northwest, was among the Mandan Indians on the Missouri River from December 29, 1797, to January 10, 1798. While there he secured data, mostly from the natives, from which he estimated the latitude and longitude of the source of the Yellowstone River. In his original manuscript journal and field note-books, containing the record of his determinations, the words "Yellow Stone" appear precisely as used by Lewis and Clark in 1805. This is, perhaps, the first use of the name in its Anglicized form, and it is certainly the first attempt to determine accurately the geographical location of the source of the stream.*

* Thompson's estimate:
  Latitude, 43° 39′ 45″ north.
  Longitude, 109° 43′ 17″ west.

3

Neither Thompson nor Lewis and Clark were originators of the name. They gave us only the English translation of a name already long in use. "This river," say Lewis and Clark, in their journal for the day of their arrival at the mouth of the now noted stream, "had been known to the French as the *Roche Jaune,* or, as we have called it, the Yellow Stone." The French name was, in fact, already firmly established among the traders and trappers of the North-west Fur Company, when Lewis and Clark met them among the Mandans. Even by the members of the expedition it seems to have been more generally used than the new English form; and the spellings, "Rejone," "Rejhone," "Rochejone," "Rochejohn," and "Rochejhone," are among their various attempts to render orthographically the French pronunciation.

Probably the name would have been adopted unchanged, as so many other French names in our geography have been, except for the recent cession of Louisiana to the United States. The policy which led the government promptly to explore, and take formal possession of its extensive acquisition, led it also, as part of the process of rapid Americanization, to give English names to all of the more prominent geographical features. In the case of the name here under consideration, this was no easy matter. The French form had already obtained wide currency, and it was reluctantly set aside for its less familiar translation. As late as 1817, it still appeared in newly English-printed books,* while among the traders and trappers of the mountains, it survived to a much later period.

Yount Peak, source of the Yellowstone (Hayden):

    Latitude, 43° 57' north.

    Longitude, 109° 52' west.

Thompson's error:

    In latitude, 17' 15".

    In longitude, 8' 43", or about 21 miles.

[The most recent U.S.G.S. quadrangle sheets give the latitude as 43° 59'N. and the longitude as 109° 52'W.—ed.]

* John Bradbury, *Travels in the Interior of America, 1809, 1810, and 1811* (London: Sherwood, Neely, and Jones, 1817). [This book is also in Reuben Gold Thwaites, *Early Western Travels*—ed.]

By whom the name *Roche Jaune,* or its equivalent form *Pierre Jaune,* was first used, it would be extremely interesting to know; but it is impossible to determine at this late day. Like their successor, "Yellow Stone," these names were not originals, but only translations. The Indian tribes along the Yellowstone and upper Missouri rivers had names for the tributary stream signifying "yellow rock,"* and the French had doubtless adopted them long before any of their number saw the stream itself.

The first explorations of the country comprised within the present limits of the State of Montana are matters of great historic uncertainty. By one account it appears that, between the years 1738 and 1753, Pierre Gaultier de Varennes, the Sieur de la Verendrye, and his sons, particularly the Chevalier de la Verendrye, conducted parties of explorers westward from Lake Superior to the Assinnaboine River, thence south to the Mandan country, and thence to the very sources of the Missouri. Even the date, January 12, 1743, is given for their first ascent of the Rocky Mountains. But such is the dearth of satisfactory evidence relating to these explorations, that positive inferences concerning them are impossible. The most that can be said is, that if De la Verendrye visited these regions, as is generally believed, to him doubtless belongs the honor of having adopted from original sources the name of the Yellowstone River.

The goal of De la Verendrye's explorations was the Pacific Ocean; but the French and Indian War, which robbed France of her dominion in America, prevented his ever reaching it. Following him, at the distance of nearly half a century, came the traders and trappers of the North-west Fur Company. As already noted, they were among the Mandans as early as 1797, and the name *Roche Jaune* was in common use among them in 1804. They appear to have been wholly ignorant of the work of De la Verendrye, and it is quite certain that, prior to 1805, none of them had reached the Yellowstone River. Lewis and

* The name "Elk River" was also used among the Crow Indians.

5

Clark particularly record the fact, while yet some distance below the junction of this river with the Missouri, that they had already passed the utmost limit of previous adventure by white men. Whatever, therefore, was at this time known of the Yellowstone could have come to these traders only from Indian sources.*

We thus find that the name, which has now become so celebrated, descends to us, through two translations, from those native races whose immemorial dwelling-place had been along the stream which it describes. What it was that led them to use the name is easily discoverable. The Yellowstone River is preeminently a river with banks of yellow rock. Along its lower course "the flood plain is bordered by high bluffs of yellow sandstone." Near the mouth of the Bighorn River stands the noted landmark, Pompey's Pillar, "a high isolated rock" of the same material. Still further up, beyond the mouth of Clark's fork, is an extensive ridge of yellow rock, the "sheer, vertical sides" of which, according to one writer, "gleam in the sunlight like massive gold." All along the lower river, in fact, from its mouth to the Great Bend at Livingston, this characteristic is more or less strikingly present.

---

* An interesting reference to the name "Yellowstone," in an entirely different quarter, occurs on Pike's map of the "Internal Provinces of Spain," published in 1810. It is a corrupt Spanish translation in the form of *"Rio de Piedro Amaretto del Missouri,"* (intended of course to be *Río de la Piedra Amarilla del Missouri*) River of the Yellow Stone of the Missouri. No clue has been discovered of the source from which Pike received this name; but the fact of its existence need occasion no surprise. The Spanish had long traded as far north as the Shoshone country, and had mingled with the French traders along the lower Missouri. Lewis and Clark found articles of their manufacture among the Shoshones in 1805. There is also limited evidence of early intercourse between them and the Crow nation. That the name of so important a stream as the Yellowstone should have become known to these traders is therefore not at all remarkable. There is, however, no reason to suppose that the Spanish translation antedates the French. It certainly plays no part in the descent of the name from the original to the English form, and it is of interest in this connection mainly as showing that, even at this early day, the name had found its way to the provinces of the south. [For a discussion of Pike's maps see Carl I. Wheat, *Mapping the Trans-Mississippi West: 1540–1861*, II, 20–25—ed.]

Whether it forms a sufficiently prominent feature of the landscape to justify christening the river from it, may appear to be open to doubt. At any rate the various descriptions of this valley by early explorers rarely refer to the same locality as being conspicuous from the presence of yellow rock. Some mention it in one place, some in another. Nowhere does it seem to have been so striking as to attract the attention of all observers. For this reason we shall go further in search of the true origin of the name, to a locality about which there can be no doubt, no difference of opinion.

Seventy-five miles below the ultimate source of the river lies the Grand Cañon of the Yellowstone, distinguished among the notable cañons of the globe by the marvelous coloring of its walls. Conspicuous among its innumerable tints is yellow. Every shade, from the brilliant plumage of the yellow bird to the rich saffron of the orange, greets the eye in bewildering profusion. There is indeed other color, unparalleled in variety and abundance, but the ever-present background of all is the beautiful fifth color of the spectrum.

So prominent is this feature that it never fails to attract attention, and all descriptions of the Cañon abound in references to it. Lieutenant Doane (1870) notes the "brilliant yellow color" of the rocks. Captain Barlow and Doctor Hayden (1871) refer, in almost the same words, to the "yellow, nearly vertical walls." Raymond (1871) speaks of the "bright yellow of the sulphury clay." Captain Jones (1873) says that "about and in the Grand Cañon the rocks are nearly all tinged a brilliant yellow." These early impressions might be repeated from the writings of every subsequent visitor who has described the scenery of the Yellowstone.

That a characteristic which so deeply moves the modern beholder should have made a profound impression on the mind of the Indian, need hardly be premised. This region was by no means unknown to him; and from the remote, although uncertain, period of his first acquaintance with it, the name of the river has undoubtedly descended.

7

Going back, then, to this obscure fountain-head, the original designation is found to have been *Mi tsi a-da-zi,** Rock Yellow River. And this, in the French tongue, became *Roche Jaune* and *Pierre Jaune;* and in English, *Yellow Rock* and *Yellow Stone*. Established usage now writes it *Yellowstone*.

* Minnetaree, one of the Siouan family of languages.

☆ 2 ☆

INDIAN OCCUPANCY OF
THE UPPER YELLOWSTONE

IT IS A SINGULAR FACT in the history of the Yellowstone National Park that no knowledge of that country seems to have
been derived from the Indians. The explanation ordinarily
advanced is that the Indians had a superstitious fear of the
geyser regions and always avoided them. How far this theory
is supported by the results of modern research is an interesting inquiry.

Three great families of Indians, the Siouan, the Algonquian,
and the Shoshonean, originally occupied the country around
the sources of the Yellowstone. Of these three families the
following tribes are alone of interest in this connection: The
Crows *(Absaroka)* of the Siouan family; the Blackfeet *(Sik-
sika)* of the Algonquian family; and the Bannocks *(Panaï'hti),*
the Eastern Shoshones, and the Sheepeaters *(Tukuarika)* of
the Shoshonean family.

The home of the Crows was in the Valley of the Yellowstone below the mountains where they have dwelt since the
white man's earliest knowledge of them. Their territory extended to the mountains which bound the Yellowstone Park
on the north and east; but they never occupied or claimed
any of the country beyond. Their well-known tribal characteristics were an insatiable love of horse-stealing and a wandering and predatory habit which caused them to roam over all
the West from the Black Hills to the Bitter Root Mountains
and from the British Possessions to the Spanish Provinces.
They were generally, although by no means always, friendly

9

to the whites, but enemies of the neighboring Blackfeet and Shoshones. Physically, they were a stalwart, handsome race, fine horsemen and daring hunters. They were every-where encountered by the trapper and prospector who generally feared them more on account of their thievish habits than for reasons of personal safety.

The Blackfeet dwelt in the country drained by the headwaters of the Missouri. Their territory was roughly defined by the Crow territory on the east and the Rocky Mountains on the west. Its southern limit was the range of mountains along the present northwest border of the Park and it extended thence to the British line. The distinguishing historic trait of these Indians was their settled hostility to their neighbors whether white or Indian. They were a tribe of perpetual fighters, justly characterized as the Ishmaelites of their race. From the day in 1806, when Captain Lewis slew one of their number, down to their final subjection by the advancing power of the whites, they never buried the hatchet. They were the terror of the trapper and miner, and hundreds of the pioneers perished at their hands. Like the Crows they were a well-developed race, good horsemen and great rovers, but, in fight, given to subterfuge and strategem rather than to open boldness of action.

In marked contrast with these warlike and wandering tribes were those of the great Shoshonean family who occupied the country around the southern, eastern, and western borders of the Park, including also that of the Park itself. The Shoshones as a family were an inferior race. They seem to have been the victims of some great misfortune which had driven them to precarious methods of subsistence and had made them the prey of their powerful and merciless neighbors. The names "Fish-eaters," "Root-diggers," and other opprobrious epithets, indicate the contempt in which they were commonly held. For the most part they had no horses, and obtained a livelihood only by the most abject means. Some of the tribes, however, rose above this degraded condition, owned horses, hunted buffalo, and met their enemies in open conflict. Such were the Bannocks and the Eastern Shoshones—tribes closely connected with the history of the Park, one occupying the country to the south-west near the Teton Mountains, and the other that to the south-east in the valley of Wind River. The Shoshones were generally friendly to the whites, and for this reason they figure less prominently in the books of early adventure than do the Crows and Blackfeet whose acts of "sanguinary violence" were a staple article for the Indian romancer.

It was an humble branch of the Shoshonean family which alone is known to have permanently occupied what is now the Yellowstone Park. They were called *Tukuarika,* or, more commonly, Sheepeaters. They were found in the Park country at the time of its discovery and had doubtless long been there. These hermits of the mountains, whom the French trappers called *"les dignes de pitié,"* have engaged the sympathy or contempt of explorers since our earliest knowledge of them. Utterly unfit for warlike contention, they seem to have sought immunity from their dangerous neighbors by dwelling among the inaccessible fastnesses of the mountains. They were destitute of even savage comforts. Their food, as their name indicates, was principally the flesh of the mountain sheep. Their clothing was composed of skins. They had no horses and were armed only with bows and arrows. They captured game by driving it into brush inclosures. Their rigorous existence left its mark on their physical nature. They were feeble in mind, diminutive in stature, and are always described as a "timid, harmless race." They may have been longer resident in this region than is commonly supposed, for there was a tradition among them, apparently connected with some remote period of geological disturbance, that most of their race were once destroyed by a terrible convulsion of nature.

Such were the Indian tribes who formerly dwelt within or near the country now embraced in the Yellowstone National Park. That the Sheepeaters actually occupied this country, and that wandering bands from other tribes occasionally visited it, there is abundant and conclusive proof. Indian trails, though

11

generally indistinct, were every-where found by the early explorers, mostly on lines since occupied by the tourist routes.* One of these followed the Yellowstone Valley entirely across the Park from north to south. It divided at Yellowstone Lake, the principal branch following the east shore, crossing Two-Ocean-Pass, and intersecting a great trail which connected the Snake and Wind River valleys. The other branch passed along the west shore of the lake and over the divide to the valleys of Snake River and Jackson Lake. This trail was intersected by an important one in the vicinity of Conant Creek leading from the Upper Snake Valley to that of Henry Fork. Other intersecting trails connected the Yellowstone River trail with the Madison and Firehole basins on the west and with the Bighorn Valley on the east.

The most important Indian trail in the Park, however, was that known as the Great Bannock Trail. It extended from Henry Lake across the Gallatin Range to Mammoth Hot Springs, where it was joined by another coming up the valley of the Gardiner. Thence it led across the Black-tail Deer Plateau to the ford above Tower Falls; and thence up the Lamar Valley, forking at Soda Butte, and reaching the Bighorn Valley by way of Clark's Fork and the Stinkingwater River.[1] This trail was certainly a very ancient and much-traveled one. It had become a deep furrow in the grassy slopes, and it is still distinctly visible in places, though unused for a quarter of a century.

Additional evidence in the same direction may be seen in the wide-spread distribution of implements peculiar to Indian use. Arrows and spear heads have been found in considerable numbers. Obsidian Cliff was an important quarry, and the open country near the outlet of Yellowstone Lake a favorite camping-ground. Certain implements, such as pipes, hammers, and stone vessels, indicating the former presence of a more civilized people, have been found to a limited extent; and some explorers have thought that a symmetrical mound in the valley of the

* See historical chart, opposite.
[1] Now more euphonistically named the Shoshone River.

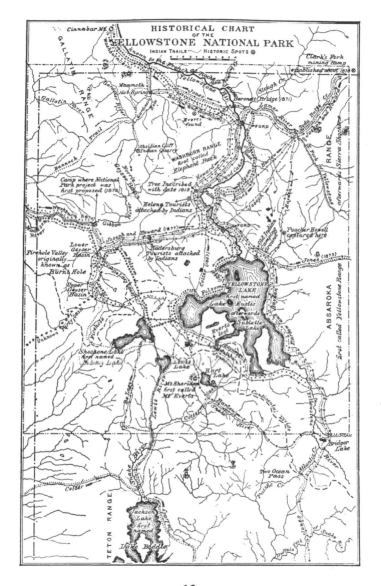

HISTORICAL CHART
OF THE
YELLOWSTONE NATIONAL PARK

INDIAN TRAILS ···· HISTORIC SPOTS ⊗

13

Snake River, below the mouth of Hart River, is of artificial origin. Reference will later be made to the discovery of a rude granite structure near the top of the Grand Teton, which is unquestionably of very ancient date.

Dr. A. C. Peale, prominently connected with the early geological explorations of this region, states that the Rustic Geyser in the Hart Lake Geyser Basin is "bordered by logs which are coated with a crystalline, semi-translucent deposit of geyserite. These logs were evidently placed around the geyser by either Indians or white men a number of years ago, as the coating is thick and the logs firmly attached to the surrounding deposit."*

More recent and perishable proofs of the presence of Indians in the Park were found by the early explorers in the rude wick-e-ups, brush inclosures, and similar contrivances of the lonely Sheepeaters; and it is not improbable that many of the arrow and spear heads were the work of these Indians.

The real question of doubt in regard to Indian occupancy of, or visits to, the Park, is therefore not one of fact, but of degree. The Sheepeaters certainly dwelt there; but as to other tribes, their acquaintance with it seems to have been limited. No word of information about the geyser regions ever fell from their lips, except that the surrounding country was known to them as the Burning Mountains. With one or two exceptions, the old trails were very indistinct, requiring an experienced eye to distinguish them from the game trails. Their undeveloped condition indicated infrequent use. Old trappers who have known this region for fifty years say that the great majority of Indians never saw it. Able Indian guides in the surrounding country became lost when they entered the Park, and the Nez Percés were forced to impress a white man as guide when they crossed the Park in 1877.

* F. V. Hayden, *Twelfth Annual Report of the United States Geological and Geographical Survey of the Territories: A Report of Progress of the Exploration in Wyoming and Idaho for the Year 1878* (Washington, Government Printing Office, 1883), I, 298. It is more than probable that this was the work of trappers.

[For a brief biography of Hayden, turn to Appendix A, VI, "Miscellaneous."—ed.]

An unknown writer, to whom extended reference will be made in a later chapter, visited the Upper Geyser Basin in 1832, accompanied by two Pend d'Oreilles Indians. Neither of these Indians had ever seen or apparently heard of the geysers, and "were quite appalled" at the sight of them, believing them to be "supernatural" and the "production of the Evil Spirit."

Lieutenant Doane, who commanded the military escort to the Yellowstone Expedition of 1870, says in his report:[*]

"Appearances indicate that the basin [of the Yellowstone Lake] had been almost entirely abandoned by the sons of the forest. A few lodges of Sheepeaters, a branch remnant of the Snake tribe, wretched beasts who run from the sight of a white man, or from any other tribe of Indians, are said to inhabit the fastnesses of the mountains around the lakes, poorly armed and dismounted, obtaining a precarious subsistence, and in a defenseless condition. We saw, however, no recent traces of them. The larger tribes never enter the basin, restrained by superstitious ideas in connection with the thermal springs."

In 1880, Col. P. W. Norris, Second Superintendent of the Park, had a long interview on the shore of the Yellowstone Lake with We-Saw, "an old but remarkably intelligent Indian" of the Shoshone tribe, who was then acting as guide to an exploring party under Governor Hoyt, of Wyoming, and who had previously passed through the Park with the expedition of 1873 under Captain W. A. Jones, U.S.A. He had also been in the Park region on former occasions. Colonel Norris records the following facts from this Indian's conversation:[†]

"We-Saw states that he had neither knowledge nor tradition of any permanent occupants of the Park save the timid Sheepeaters. . . . He said that his people (Shoshones) the Bannocks and the Crows, occasionally visited the Yellowstone Lake and River portions of the Park, but very seldom the

[*] Lieutenant Gustav C. Doane, *Report Upon the Yellowstone Expedition of 1870* (Washington, Government Printing Office, 1871), 26.

[†] P. W. Norris, *Annual Report of the Superintendent of the Yellowstone National Park for 1881* (Washington, Government Printing Office, 1882), 38.

geyser regions, which he declared were *'heap, heap, bad,'* and never wintered there, as white men sometimes did with horses."

It seems that even the resident Sheepeaters knew little of the geyser basins. General Sheridan, who entered the Park from the south in 1882, makes this record in his report of the expedition:*

"We had with us five Sheep Eating Indians as guides, and, strange to say, although these Indians had lived for years and years about Mounts Sheridan and Hancock, and the high mountains south-east of the Yellowstone Lake, they knew nothing about the Firehole Geyser Basin, and they exhibited more astonishment and wonder than any of us."

Evidence like the foregoing clearly indicates that this country was *terra incognita* to the vast body of Indians who dwelt around it, and again this singular fact presents itself for explanation. Was it, as is generally supposed, a "superstitious fear" that kept them away? The incidents just related give some color to such a theory; but if it were really true we should expect to find well authenticated Indian traditions of so marvelous a country. Unfortunately, history records none. It is not meant by this to imply that reputed traditions concerning the Yellowstone are unknown. For instance, it is related that the Crows always refused to tell the whites of the geysers because they believed that whoever visited them became endowed with supernatural powers, and they wished to retain a monopoly of this knowledge. But traditions of this sort, like most Indian curiosities now offered for sale, are evidently of spurious origin. Only in the names "Yellowstone" and "Burning Mountains" do we find any original evidence that this land of wonders appealed in the least degree to the native imagination.

The real explanation of this remarkable ignorance appears to us to rest on grounds essentially practical. There was nothing to induce the Indians to visit the Park country. For three-

* Lieutenant General P. H. Sheridan, *Exploration of Parts of Wyoming, Idaho, and Montana, in 1882* (Washington, Government Printing Office, 1882), 11.

fourths of the year that country is inaccessible on account of snow. It is covered with dense forests, which in most places are so filled with fallen timber and tangled underbrush as to be practically impassable. As a game country in those early days it could not compare with the lower surrounding valleys. As a highway of communication between the valleys of the Missouri, Snake, Yellowstone, and Bighorn rivers, it was no thoroughfare. The great routes, except the Bannock Trail already described, lay on the outside. All the conditions, therefore, which might attract the Indians to this region were wanting. Even those sentimental influences, such as a love of sublime scenery and a curiosity to see the strange freaks of nature, evidently had less weight with them than with their pale-face brethren.

Summarizing the results of such knowledge, confessedly meager, as exists upon this subject, it appears:

(1) That the country now embraced in the Yellowstone National Park was occupied, at the time of its discovery, by small bands of Sheepeater Indians, probably not exceeding in number one hundred and fifty souls. They dwelt in the neighborhood of the Washburn and Absaroka Ranges, and among the mountains around the sources of the Snake. They were not familiar with the geyser regions.

(2) Wandering bands from other tribes occasionally visited this country, but generally along the line of the Yellowstone River or the Great Bannock Trail. Their knowledge of the geyser regions was extremely limited, and very few had ever seen or heard of them. It is probable that the Indian visited this country more frequently in earlier times than since the advent of the white man.

(3) The Indians avoided the region of the Upper Yellowstone from practical, rather than from sentimental, considerations.[2]

The legal processes by which the vast territory of these

[2] Dr. Merrill D. Beal disagrees. He believes that the shores of the lakes of the Yellowstone were teeming with Indians every summer. *The Story of Man in Yellowstone,* 84–91.

various tribes passed to the United States, are full of incongruities resulting from a general ignorance of the country in question. By the Treaty of Fort Laramie, dated September 17, 1851, between the United States on the one hand, and the Crows, Blackfeet, and other northern tribes on the other, the Crows were given, as part of their territory, all that portion of the Park country which lies east of the Yellowstone River; and the Blackfeet, all that portion lying between the Yellowstone River and the Continental Divide. This was before any thing whatever was known of the country so given away. None of the Shoshone tribes were party to the treaty, and the rights of the Sheepeaters were utterly ignored. That neither the Blackfeet nor the Crows had any real claim to these extravagant grants is evidenced by their prompt relinquishment of them in the first subsequent treaties. Thus, by treaty of October 17, 1855, the Blackfeet agreed that all of their portion of the Park country, with much other territory, should be and remain a common hunting ground for certain designated tribes; and by treaty of May 17, 1868, the Crows relinquished all of their territory south of the Montana boundary line.

That portion of the Park country drained by the Snake River was always considered Shoshone territory, although apparently never formally recognized in any public treaty. By an unratified treaty, dated September 24, 1868, the provisions of which seem to have been the basis of subsequent arrangements with the Shoshonean tribes, all this territory and much besides was ceded to the United States, and the tribes were located upon small reservations.

It thus appears that at the time the Park was created, March 1, 1872, all the territory included in its limits had been ceded to the United States except the hunting ground above referred to, and the narrow strip of Crow territory east of the Yellowstone where the north boundary of the Park lies two or three miles north of the Montana line. The "hunting ground" arrangement was abrogated by statute of April 15, 1874, and the strip of Crow territory was purchased under an agreement with the Crows, dated June 12, 1880, and ratified by Congress, April 11, 1882, thus extinguishing the last remaining Indian title to any portion of the Yellowstone Park.

JOHN COLTER

Lewis and Clark passed the second winter of their expedition at the mouth of the Columbia River. In the spring and summer of 1806 they accomplished their return to St. Louis. Upon their arrival at the site of their former winter quarters among the Mandans, an incident occurred which forms the initial point in the history of the Yellowstone National Park. It is thus recorded in the journal of the expedition under date of August 14 and 15, 1806:*

"In the evening we were applied to by one of our men, Colter, who was desirous of joining the two trappers who had accompanied us, and who now proposed an expedition up the river, in which they were to find traps and give him a share of the profits. The offer was a very advantageous one, and, as he had always performed his duty, and his services might be dispensed with, we agreed that he might go provided none of the rest would ask or expect a similar indulgence. To this they cheerfully answered that they wished Colter every success and would not apply for liberty to separate before we reached St. Louis. We therefore supplied him, as did his comrades also, with powder, lead, and a variety of articles which might be useful to him, and he left us the next day."

To our explorers, just returning from a two years' sojourn in the wilderness, Colter's decision seemed too remarkable to be passed over in silence. The journal continues:

"The example of this man shows us how easily men may be

* Elliott Coues, *The History of the Expedition Under the Command of Lewis and Clark*, III, 1181–82.

weaned from the habits of civilized life to the ruder but scarcely less fascinating manners of the woods. This hunter has now been absent for many years from the frontiers, and might naturally be presumed to have some anxiety, or some curiosity at least, to return to his friends and his country; yet just at the moment when he is approaching the frontiers, he is tempted by a hunting scheme to give up those delightful prospects, and go back without the least reluctance to the solitude of the woods."

Colter seems to have stood well in the esteem of his officers. Besides the fair character given him in his discharge, the record of the expedition shows that he was frequently selected when one or two men were required for important special duty. That he had a good eye for topography may be inferred from the fact that Captain Clark, several years after the expedition was over, placed upon his map certain important information on the strength of Colter's statements, who alone had traversed the region in question. In another instance, when Bradbury, the English naturalist, was about to leave St. Louis to join the Astorians in the spring of 1811, Clark referred him to Colter, who had returned from the mountains, as a person who could conduct him to a certain natural curiosity on the Missouri some distance above St. Charles. Colter had not seen the place for six years. In the *Missouri Gazette,* for April 18, 1811, he is referred to as a "celebrated hunter and woodsman." These glimpses of his record, and a remarkable incident to be related further on, clearly indicate that he was a man of superior mettle to that of the average hunter and trapper.

Colter's whereabouts during the three years following his discharge are difficult to fix upon. It may, however, be set down as certain that he and his companions ascended the Yellowstone River, not the Missouri. Captain Clark's return journey down the first-mentioned stream had made known to them that it was better beaver country than the Missouri, and Colter's subsequent wanderings clearly indicate that his base of operations was in the valley of the Yellowstone near the mouth of the Bighorn, Pryor's Fork, or other tributary stream.

21

In the summer of 1807, he made an expedition, apparently alone, although probably in company with Indians, which has given him title to a place in the history of the Yellowstone Park, and which was destined in later years to assume an importance little enough suspected by him at the time. His route appears upon Lewis and Clark's map of 1814, and is there called "Colter's route in 1807." There is no note or explanation, and we are left to retrace, on the basis of a dotted line, a few names, and a date, one of those singular individual wanderings through the wilderness which now and then find a permanent place in history.

The "route," as traced on the map, starts from a point on Pryor's Fork, the first considerable tributary of the Yellowstone above the mouth of the Bighorn. Colter's intention seems to have been to skirt the eastern base of the Absaroka Range until he should reach an accessible pass across the mountains of which the Indians had probably told him; then to cross over to the headwaters of Pacific or gulf-flowing streams; and then to return by way of the Upper Yellowstone.

Accordingly, after he had passed through Pryor's Gap, he took a south-westerly direction as far as Clark's Fork, which stream he ascended for some distance, and then crossed over to the Stinkingwater. Here he discovered a large boiling spring, strongly impregnated with tar and sulphur, the odor of which, perceptible for a great distance around, has given the stream its "unhappy name."[1]

From this point Colter continued along the eastern flank of the Absaroka Range, fording the several tributaries of the Bighorn River which flow down from that range, and finally came to the upper course of the main stream now known as Wind River. He ascended this stream to its source, crossing the divide in the vicinity of Lincoln or Union Pass, and found himself upon the Pacific slope. The map clearly shows that at this point he had reached what the Indians called the "summit of the world" near by the sources of all great streams of the west. That he discovered one of the easy passes between

[1] A marker just outside of Cody, Wyoming, identifies the probable site.

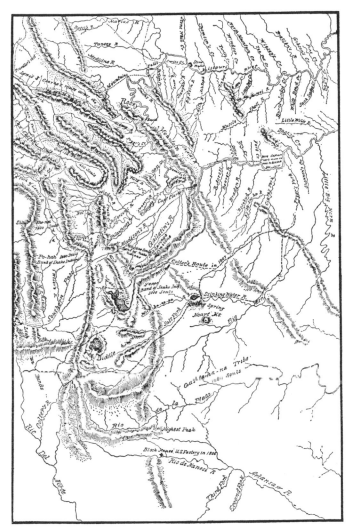

COLTER'S ROUTE IN 1807

[This map is a portion of the Lewis and Clark map of 1814. A full reproduction is in Carl I. Wheat, *Mapping the Trans-Mississippi West: 1540–1861*, II, facing p. 57.]

Wind River and the Pacific slope, is evident from the reference in the *Missouri Gazette* already alluded to and here reproduced for the first time. It is from the pen of a Mr. H. M. Brackenridge, a contemporary writer of note on topics of western adventure. It reads:

"At the head of the Gallatin Fork, and of the Grosse Corne of the Yellowstone [the Bighorn River], from discoveries since the voyage of Lewis and Clark, it is found less difficult to cross than the Allegheny Mountains. Coulter, a celebrated hunter and woodsman, informed me that a loaded wagon would find no obstruction in passing."

The "discoveries" are of course those of Colter, for no other white man at this time had been in those parts.

From the summit of the mountains he descended to the westward; crossed the Snake River and Teton Pass to Pierre's Hole, and then turned north, recrossing the Teton Range by the Indian trail in the valley of what is now Conant Creek, just north of Jackson Lake.* Thence he continued his course until he reached Yellowstone Lake,† at some point along its southwestern shore. He passed around the west shore to the northernmost point of the Thumb, and then resumed his northerly course over the hills arriving at the Yellowstone River in the valley of Alum Creek. He followed the left bank of the river to the ford just above Tower Falls, where the great Bannock Trail used to cross, and then followed this trail to its junction with his outward route on Clark's Fork. From this point he re-crossed to the Stinkingwater, possibly in order to re-visit the strange phenomena there, but more probably to explore new trapping territory on his way back. He descended the Stinkingwater until about south of Pryor's Gap, when he turned north and shortly after arrived at his starting point.

* For the names given by Captain Clark to these bodies of water, see Appendix A, "Jackson Lake" and "Yellowstone Lake."

† In adopting, as Colter's point of crossing the Yellowstone, the ford at Tower Creek, the author has followed the Hon. N. P. Langford, in his reprint of Folsom's *Valley of the Upper Yellowstone* (St. Paul, 1894). All other writers who have touched upon the subject have assumed the ford to be that near the Mud Geyser.

The direction of Colter's progress, as here indicated, and the identification of certain geographical features noted by him, differ somewhat from the ordinary interpretation of that adventure. But, while it would be absurd to dogmatize upon so uncertain a subject, it is believed that the theory adopted is fairly well supported by the facts as now known. It must in the first place be assumed that Colter exercised ordinary common sense upon this journey and availed himself of all information that could facilitate his progress. It is probable that he was under the guidance of Indians who knew the country; but if not, he frequently stopped, like any traveler in an unknown region, to inquire his way. He sought the established trails, low mountain passes, and well-known fords, and did not, as the map suggests, take a direction that would carry him through the very roughest and most impassable mountain country on the continent. It is necessary to orient his map so as to make both his outgoing and return routes extend nearly due north and south, instead of north-east and south-west, in order to reconcile his geography at all with the modern maps. With these precautions some of the difficulty of the situation disappears.

Colter, it is therefore assumed, followed the great trail along the Absurokas to the Wind River Valley, and crossed the divide by one of the easy passes at its head. His two crossings of the Teton Range were along established trails. He evidently lost his bearings somewhat in the vicinity of the Yellowstone Lake, but as soon as he arrived at the river below the lake he kept along the trail until he reached the important crossing at Tower Falls. If he was in company with Indians who had ever been through that country before, he learned that it would be no advantage to cross at Mud Geyser, inasmuch as he would strike the Great Bannock Trail at the next ford below. Moreover, the distance below the lake to the point where Colter touched the Yellowstone is clearly greater than that to the Mud Geyser Ford. The bend in the river at the Great Falls, and the close proximity of the Washburn Range to the river, are distinctly indicated. The locality noted on the map as "Hot

25

Springs Brimstone" is evidently not that near the Mud Geyser, as generally assumed, but instead, that of the now world-renowned Mammoth Hot Springs. As will be seen from the map, it is nearer the Gallatin River than it is to the Yellowstone *where Colter crossed.* If Colter visited the Springs from Tower Falls, as is not unlikely, a clue is supplied to the otherwise perplexing reference to the Gallatin River in the above extract from the *Missouri Gazette,* for it would thus appear that he was near the sources of both the Grosse Corne and of the Gallatin.

The essential difficulties in the way of this theory (and they exist with any possible theory that can be advanced) are the following: (1) There is no stream on the map that can stand for the Snake River either above or below Jackson Lake, although Colter must have crossed it in each place. "Colter's River" comes nearest the first location, and may possibly be intended to represent that stream; but Clark's evident purpose to drain Jackson Lake into the Bighorn River doubtless led to a distortion of the map in his locality. (2) The erroneous shape given to the Yellowstone Lake will be readily understood by anyone who has visited its western shore. The jutting promontories to the eastward entirely conceal from view the great body of the lake and give it a form not unlike that upon Clark's map. (3) The absence of the Great Falls from the map is not easily accounted for, although the location and trend of the Grand Cañon are shown with remarkable accuracy. (4) The absence of the many hot springs districts, through which Colter passed, particularly that at the west end of the Yellowstone Lake, may be explained by the same spirit of incredulity which led to the rejection of all similar accounts for a period of more than sixty years. It is probable that Clark was not willing to recognize Colter's statements on this subject further than to note on his map the location of the most wonderful of the hot springs groups mentioned by him.

The direction in which Colter traveled is a matter of no essential importance, and that here adopted is based solely upon the consideration that the doubling of the trail upon itself between Clark's Fork and the Stinkingwater River, and the erratic course of the route around Yellowstone Lake, can not be well accounted for on the contrary hypothesis.*

Such, in the main, is "Colter's route in 1807." That he was the discoverer of Yellowstone Lake, and the foremost herald of the strange phenomena of that region, may be accepted as beyond question. He did not, as is generally supposed, see the Firehole Geyser basins. But he saw too much for his reputation as a man of veracity. No author or map-maker would jeopardize the success of his work by incorporating in it such incredible material as Colter furnished. His stories were not believed; their author became the subject of jest and ridicule; and the region of his adventures was long derisively known as "Colter's Hell."[2]

The story of Colter's subsequent experience before he returned to St. Louis is thrilling in the extreme. Although it has no direct bearing upon this narrative, still, since it is part of the biography of the discoverer of the Upper Yellowstone, it can not be omitted. The detailed account we owe to the naturalist Bradbury, already referred to. He saw Colter above St. Louis in the spring of 1811, one year after his return from the mountains, and received the story directly from him. All other accounts are variations from Bradbury. Irving, who has made this story an Indian classic, borrows it *in toto*. Perhaps in all the records of Indian adventure there is not another instance of such a miraculous escape, in which the details are throughout so clearly within the range of possibility. It is a consistent narrative from beginning to end. In briefest outline it is as follows:

* This name early came to be restricted to the locality where Colter discovered the tar spring on the Stinkingwater, probably because few trappers ever saw the other similar localities visited by him. But Colter's descriptions, so well summed up by Irving in his *Captain Bonneville*, undoubtedly refer in large part to what he saw in the Yellowstone and Snake River valleys.

2 Chittenden here depended upon the Lewis and Clark map of 1814, which was entirely erroneous in the western part where Colter's trail is traced. See the leading authority on Colter, Merrill Mattes, *Behind the Legend of Colter's Hell: The Early Exploration of Yellowstone National Park,* and Beal, *The Story of Man in Yellowstone,* 30–51, 285–98. Chittenden changed his narration in subsequent works. Certainly there is as much evidence that Colter did get to the Yellowstone as that he did not.

When Colter returned from his expedition of 1807, he found Manuel Lisa, of the Missouri Fur Company, already in the country, where he had just arrived from St. Louis. With him was one Potts, believed to be the same person who had been a private in the party of Lewis and Clark. In the spring of 1808, Colter and his old companion in arms set out to the headwaters of the Missouri on a trapping expedition. It was on a branch of Jefferson Fork that they went to work, and here they met with their disastrous experience.

One morning while they were in a canoe examining their traps they were surprised by a large party of Blackfeet Indians. Potts attempted resistance and was slain on the spot. Colter, with more presence of mind, gave himself up as the only possible chance of avoiding immediate death. The Indians then consulted as to how they should kill him in order to yield themselves the greatest amount of amusement. Colter, upon being questioned as to his fleetness of foot, sagaciously replied that he was a poor runner (though in fact very swift), and the Indians, believing that it would be a safe experiment, decided that he should run for his life. Accordingly he was stripped naked and was led by the chief to a point three or four hundred yards in advance of the main body of the Indians. Here he was told *"to save himself if he could,"* and the race began—one man against five hundred.

The Indians quickly saw how they had been outwitted, for Colter flew away from them as if upon the wings of the wind. But his speed cost him dear. The exertion caused the blood to stream from his mouth and nostrils, and run down over his naked form. The prickly pear and rough ground lacerated his feet. Six miles away across a level plain was a fringe of cottonwood on the banks of the Jefferson River. Short of that lay not a shadow of chance of concealment. It was a long race, but life hung upon the issue. The Indians had not counted on such prodigious running. Gradually they fell off, and when Colter ventured for the first time to glance back, only a small number were in his wake. Encouragement was now added to hope, and he ran even faster than before.

But there was one Indian who was too much for him. He was steadily shortening the distance between them, and at last had arrived within a spear's throw. Was Colter to be slain by a single Indian after having distanced five hundred? He would see. Suddenly whirling about, he confronted the Indian, who was astounded at the sudden move and at Colter's bloody appearance. He tried to hurl his spear but stumbled and broke it as he fell. Colter seized the pointed portion and pinned the Indian to the earth.

Again he resumed his flight. He reached the Jefferson, and discovered, some distance below, a raft of driftwood against the head of an island. He dived under this raft and found a place where he could get his head above water. There, in painful suspense, he awaited developments. The Indians explored the island and examined the raft, but Colter's audacious spirit was beyond their comprehension. It did not occur to them that he was all the time surveying their movements from his hiding place under the timber, and they finally abandoned the search and withdrew. Colter had saved himself. When evening came he swam several miles down the river and then went ashore. For seven days he wandered naked and unarmed, over stones, cacti, and the prickly pear, scorched by the heat of noon and chilled by the frost of night, finding his sole subsistence in such roots as he might dig, until at last he reached Lisa's trading post on the Bighorn River.[3]

Even this terrible adventure could not dismay the dauntless Colter, and he remained still another year in the mountains. Finally, in the spring of 1810, he got into a canoe and dropped down the river, "three thousand miles in thirty days,"[4] reaching St. Louis, May 1, after an absence of six years.

Colter remained in St. Louis for a time giving Clark what information he could concerning the places he had seen, and evidently talking a great deal about his adventures. Finally he

[3] While the story here related is considered true, Chittenden's chronology is wrong. Colter explored Yellowstone *after* joining Lisa, and his experience with the Blackfeet followed his Yellowstone exploration. Beal, *The Story of Man in Yellowstone*, 36ff.

[4] Twenty-five hundred miles would be more correct.

retired to the country some distance up the Missouri and married. Here we again catch a glimpse of him when the Astorians were on their way up the river. As Colter saw the well appointed expedition setting out for the mountains, the old fever seized him again and he was upon the point of joining the party. But what the hardships of the wilderness and the pleasures of civilization could not dissuade him from doing, the charms of a newly-married wife easily accomplished. Colter remained behind; and here the curtain of oblivion falls upon the discoverer of the Yellowstone. It is not without genuine satisfaction that, having followed him through the incredible mazes of "Colter's Hell," we bid him adieu amid surroundings of so different a character.

☆ 4 ☆

THE TRADER AND TRAPPER

FOR SIXTY YEARS after Lewis and Clark returned from their expedition, the headwaters of the Yellowstone remained unexplored except by the trader and trapper. The traffic in peltries it was that first induced extensive exploration of the West. Concerning the precious metals, the people seem to have had little faith in their abundant existence in the West, and no organized search for them was made in the earlier years of the century. But that country, even in its unsettled state, had other and important sources of wealth. Myriads of beaver inhabited the streams and innumerable buffalo roamed the valleys. The buffalo furnished the trapper with means of subsistence, and beaver furs were better than mines of gold. Far in advance of the tide of settlement the lonely trapper, and after him the trader, penetrated the unknown West. Gradually the enterprise of individuals crystallized around a few important nuclei and there grew up those great fur-trading companies which for many years exercised a kind of paternal sway over the Indians and the scarcely more civilized trappers. A brief résumé of the history of these companies will show how important a place they occupy in the early history of the Upper Yellowstone.

The climax of the western fur business may be placed at about the year 1830. At that time three great companies operated in territories whose converging lines of separation centered in the region about Yellowstone Lake. The oldest and most important of them, and the one destined to outlive the others, was the world-renowned Hudson's Bay Company. It was at that time more than a century and a half old. Its earlier

31

history was in marked contrast with that of later years. Secure in the monopoly which its extensive charter rights guaranteed, it had been content with substantial profits and had never pushed its business far into new territory nor managed it with aggressive vigor. It was not until forced to action by the encroachments of a dangerous rival, that it became the prodigious power of later times.

This rival was the great North-west Fur Company of Montreal. It had grown up since the French and Indian War, partly as a result of that conflict, and finally took corporate form in 1787. It had none of the important territorial rights of the Hudson's Bay Company, but its lack of monopoly was more than made up by the enterprise of its promoters. With its bands of Canadian frontiersmen, it boldly penetrated the northwest and paid little respect to those territorial rights which its venerable rival was powerless to enforce. It rapidly extended its operations far into the unexplored interior. Lewis and Clark found its traders among the Mandans in 1804. In 1811 the Astorians saw its first party descend the Columbia to the sea. Two years later the American traders on the Pacific Coast were forced to succumb to their British rivals.

A long and bitter strife now ensued between the two British companies. It even assumed the magnitude of civil war, and finally resulted in a frightful massacre of unoffending colonists. The British government interfered and forced the rivals into court, where they were brought to the verge of ruin by protracted litigation. A compromise was at last effected in 1821 by an amalgamation of the two companies under the name of the older rival.

But in the meantime a large part of their best fur country had been lost. In 1815 the government of the United States excluded British traders from its territory east of the Rocky Mountains. To the west of this limit, however, the amalgamated company easily forced all its rivals from the field. No American fur company ever attained the splendid organization, nor the influence over the Indians, possessed by the Hudson's Bay Company. At the time of which we write it was master of the trade in the Columbia River Valley, and the eastern limit of its operations within the territory of the United States was nearly coincident with the present western boundary of the Yellowstone Park.

The second of the great companies to which reference has been made was the American Fur Company. It was the final outcome of John Jacob Astor's various attempts to control the fur trade of the United States. Although it was incorporated in 1809, it was for a time overshadowed by the more brilliant enterprises known as the Pacific Fur Company and the Southwest Fur Company. The history of Mr. Astor's Pacific Fur Company, the dismal experiences of the Astorians, and the deplorable failure of the whole undertaking, are matters familiar to all readers of Irving's *Astoria*.

The other project gave for a time more substantial promise of success. A British company of considerable importance, under the name of the Mackinaw Company, with headquarters at Michilimacinac, had for some time operated in the country about the headwaters of the Mississippi now included in the states of Wisconsin and Minnesota. Astor succeeded in forming a new company, partly with American and partly with Canadian capital. This company bought out the Mackinaw Company, and changed the name to South-west Fur Company. But scarcely had its promising career begun when it was cut short by the War of 1812.

The failure of these two attempts caused Mr. Astor to turn to the old American Fur Company. The exclusion Act of 1815 enabled him to buy at his own price the North-west Fur Company's posts on the upper rivers, and the American Company rapidly extended its trade over all the country, from Lake Superior to the Rocky Mountains. Its posts multiplied in every direction, and at an early date steamboats began to do its business up the Missouri River from St. Louis. It gradually absorbed lesser concerns, such as the Missouri Fur Company, and the Columbia Fur Company, and in 1823 was reorganized under the name of The North American Fur Company. In 1834, Astor sold his interests to Chouteau, Valle and Company, of St. Louis, and retired from the business. At this time the general western limit of the territory operated in by this formidable company was the northern and eastern slope of the mountains which bound the Yellowstone Park on the north and east. Its line of operations was down the river to St. Louis, and its great trading posts were located at frequent intervals between.

The third of the great rival companies was the Rocky Mountain Fur Company, which originated in St. Louis in 1822, and received its full organization in 1826 under the direction of Jedediah Smith, David Jackson, and William Sublette. Among the leading spirits, who at one time or another guided its affairs, was the famous mountaineer James Bridger to whom frequent reference will be made.

This company had its general center of operations on the head waters of Green River to the west of South Pass. Unlike the other companies, it had no navigable stream along which it could establish posts and conduct its operations. By the necessities of its exclusively mountain trade it developed a new feature of the fur business. The *voyageur,* with his canoe and oar, gave way to the mountaineer, with his saddle and rifle. The trading post was replaced by the annual rendezvous, which was in many points the forerunner of the later cattle "round-ups" of the plains. These rendezvous were agreed upon each year at localities best suited for the convenience of the trade. Hither in the spring came from the east convoys of supplies for the season's use. Hither repaired also the various parties of hunters and trappers and such bands of Indians as roamed in the vicinity. These meetings were great occasions, both in the transactions of business and in the round of festivities that always prevailed. After the traffic of the occasion was over, and the plans for the ensuing year were agreed upon, the convoys returned to the States and the trappers to their retreats in the mountains. The field of operations of this company was very extensive and included about all of the West not controlled by the Hudson's Bay and American Fur Companies.

Thus was the territory of the great West practically parceled

34

out among these three companies.* It must not be supposed that there was any agreement, tacit or open, that each company should keep within certain limits. There were, indeed, a few temporary arrangements of this sort, but for the most part each company maintained the right to work in any territory it saw fit, and there was constant invasion by each of the proper territories of the other. But the practical necessities of the business kept them, broadly speaking, within the limits which we have noted. The roving bands of "free trappers" and "lone traders," and individual expeditions like those of Captain Bonneville and Nathaniel J. Wyeth, acknowledged allegiance to none of the great organizations, but wandered where they chose, dealing by turns with each of the companies.

Nor did any company maintain an exclusive monopoly of its peculiar methods of conducting business. The American Fur Company frequently held rendezvous at points remote from its trading posts; and the Rocky Mountain Fur Company in later years resorted to the Missouri River as its line of supplies. In fact, the interests of the two companies finally became to such an extent dependent upon each other that a union was effected, in 1839, under the firm name of P. Chouteau, Jr.

The records of those early days abound in references to the fierce competition in trade which existed between these great organizations. It led to every manner of device or subterfuge which might deceive a rival as to routes, conceal from him important trapping grounds, undermine the loyalty of his employes or excite the hostility of the Indians against him. It often led to deeds of violence, and made the presence of a rival band of trappers more dreaded than a war party of the implacable Blackfeet.

The vigor and enterprise of these traders caused their busi-

* A singular and striking coincidence at once discloses itself to any one who compares maps showing the territories operated in by these three companies, and those which belonged to the three great families of Indians mentioned in a preceding chapter. By far the larger part of the Hudson's Bay Company's territory, as far west as the main range of the Rocky Mountains, was Algonquian. The American Fur Company's territory was almost entirely Siouan, and that of the Rocky Mountain Fur Company, Shoshonean.

35

ness to penetrate the remotest and most inaccessible corners of the land. Silliman's Journal for January, 1834, declares that:

"The mountains and forests, from the Arctic Sea to the Gulf of Mexico, are threaded through every maze by the hunter. Every river and tributary stream, from the Columbia to the Rio del Norte, and from the Mackenzie to the Colorado of the West, from their head waters to their junctions are searched and trapped for beaver."

That a business of such all-pervading character should have left a region like our present Yellowstone Park unexplored would seem extremely doubtful. That region lay, a sort of neutral ground, between the territories of the rival fur companies. Its streams abounded with beaver; and, although hemmed in by vast mountains, and snow-bound most of the year, it could not have escaped discovery. In fact, every part of it was repeatedly visited by trappers. Rendezvous were held on every side of it, and once, it is believed, in Hayden Valley, just north of Yellowstone Lake.[1] Had the fur business been more enduring, the geyser regions would have become known at least a generation sooner.

But a business carried on with such relentless vigor naturally soon taxed the resources of nature beyond its capacity for reproduction. In regions under the control of a single organization, as in the vast domains of the Hudson's Bay Company, great care was taken to preserve the fur-bearing animals from extinction; but in United States territory, the exigencies of competition made any such provision impossible. The poor beaver, as at a later day the buffalo, quickly succumbed to his ubiquitous enemies. There was no spot remote enough for him to build his dam in peace, and the once innumerable multitude speedily dwindled away. The few years immediately preceding and following 1830 were the halcyon days of the fur trade in the United States. Thenceforward it rapidly declined, and by 1850 had shrunk to a mere shadow of its former greatness. With its disappearance the early knowledge of the Upper

[1] Merrill Mattes gives strong arguments against a rendezvous ever being held in Yellowstone. *Behind the Legend of Colter's Hell,* 273.

Yellowstone also disappeared. Subsequent events—the Mormon emigration, the war with Mexico, and the discovery of gold—drew attention, both private and official, in other directions; and the great wonderland became again almost as much unknown as in the days of Lewis and Clark.

☆ 5 ☆

EARLY KNOWLEDGE OF THE YELLOWSTONE

ON THE WEST BANK of the Yellowstone River, a quarter of a mile above the Upper Falls, in a ravine now crossed by a lofty wooden bridge, stands a pine tree, on which is the oldest record, except that of Colter, of the presence of white men within the present limits of the Park. It is an inscription, giving the initials of a name and the date when inscribed. It was discovered in 1880 by Col. P. W. Norris, then superintendent of the Park. It is now practically illegible from overgrowth, although some of the characters can still be made out. Col. Norris, who saw it fifteen years ago, claims to have successfully deciphered it. He verified the date by counting the annual rings on another tree near by, which bore hatchet marks, presumably of the same date. The time that had elapsed since these cuts were made corresponded well with the inscribed date. The inscription was:

J O R
Aug 19 1819

Efforts have been made to trace this inscription to some of the early noted trappers, but the attempt can hardly succeed. Even if an identity of initials were established, the identity of individuals would still remain in doubt. Nothing short of some authentic record of such a visit as must have taken place can satisfy the requirements of the case. In the absence of any such record, the most that can be said is that the inscription is proof positive that the Park country was visited by white men, after Colter's time, fully fifty years before its final discovery.

Col. Norris' researches disclosed other similar evidence, although in no other instance with so plain a clue as to date. Near Beaver Lake and Obsidian Cliff, he found, in 1878, a cache of marten traps of an old pattern used by the Hudson's Bay Company's trappers fifty years before. He also examined the ruins of an ancient block-house discovered by Frederick Bottler at the base of Mt. Washburn, near the Grand Cañon of the Yellowstone. Its decayed condition indicated great age. In other places, the stumps of trees, old logs used to cross streams, and many similar proofs, were brought to light by that inveterate ranger of the wilderness.

The Washburn party, in 1870, discovered on the east bank of the Yellowstone, just above Mud Geyser, the remains of a pit, probably once used for concealment in shooting water fowl.

In 1882, there was still living in Montana, at the advanced age of one hundred and two years, a Frenchman by the name of Baptiste Ducharne. This man spent the summers of 1824 and 1826 on the Upper Yellowstone River trapping for beaver. He saw the Grand Cañon and Falls of the Yellowstone and the Yellowstone Lake. He passed through the geyser regions, and could accurately describe them more than half a century after he had seen them.

A book called *The River of the West,** published in 1871, but copyrighted in 1869, before the publication of any modern account of the geyser regions, contains the record of an adventure in the Yellowstone three years after those of Ducharne. The book is a biography of one Joseph Meek, a trapper and pioneer of considerable note. The adventure to which reference is made took place in 1829, and was the result of a decision by the Rocky Mountain Fur Company to retire from competition with the Hudson's Bay Company in the Snake River Valley. In leaving the country, Captain William Sublette, the chief partner, led his party up Henry Fork, across the Madison and Gallatin rivers, to the high ridge overlooking the Yellowstone, at some point near the present Cinnabar Mountain.

* Francis Fuller Victor, *The River of the West,* 75–76.

Here the party was dispersed by a band of Blackfeet, and Meek, one of its members, became separated from his companions. He had lost his horse and most of his equipment and in this condition he wandered for several days, without food or shelter, until he was found by two of his companions. His route lay in a southerly direction, to the eastward of the Yellowstone, at some distance back from the river. On the morning of the fifth day he had the following experience:

"Being desirous to learn something of the progress he had made, he ascended a low mountain in the neighborhood of his camp, and behold! the whole country beyond was smoking with vapor from boiling springs, and burning with gases issuing from small craters, each of which was emitting a sharp, whistling sound. When the first surprise of this astonishing scene had passed, Joe began to admire its effect from an artistic point of view. The morning being clear, with a sharp frost, he thought himself reminded of the City of Pittsburg, as he had beheld it on a winter morning, a couple of years before. This, however, related only to the rising smoke and vapor; for the extent of the volcanic region was immense, reaching far out of sight. The general face of the country was smooth and rolling, being a level plain, dotted with cone-shaped mounds. On the summit of these mounds were small craters from four to eight feet in diameter. Interspersed among these on the level plain were larger craters, some of them from four to six miles across. Out of these craters, issued blue flames and molten brimstone."*

Making some allowance for the trapper's tendency to exaggeration, we recognize in this description the familiar picture of the hot springs districts. The precise location is difficult to determine; but Meek's previous wanderings, and the subsequent route of himself and his companions whom he met here, show conclusively that it was one of the numerous districts east of the Yellowstone, which were possibly then more active than now.

This book affords much other evidence of early knowledge

* *Ibid.*, 75.

40

of the country immediately bordering the present Park. The Great Bend of the Yellowstone where Livingston now stands, was already a famous rendezvous. The Gardiner and Firehole Rivers were well known to trappers; and a much-used trail led from the Madison across the Gallatin Range to the Gardiner, and thence up the Yellowstone and East Fork across the mountains to the Bighorn Valley.

In Vol. I, No 17, August 13, 1842, of *The Wasp,* a Mormon paper published at Nauvoo, Ill., occurs the first, as it is by far the best, of all early accounts of the geyser regions prior to 1870. It is an extract from an unpublished work, entitled "Life in the Rocky Mountains." Who was the author will probably never be known; but that he was a man of culture and education, altogether beyond the average trader, is evident from the passing glimpse which we have of his work.[1] He apparently made his visit from some point in the valley of Henry Fork not far west of the Firehole River, for, at the utmost allowance, he traveled only about sixty or seventy miles to reach the geyser basins. The evidence is conclusive that the scene of this visit was the Upper Geyser Basin. It fits perfectly with the description, while numerous insuperable discrepancies render identification with the Lower Basin, which some have sought to establish, impossible. Following is this writer's narrative:

"I had heard in the summer of 1833, while at rendezvous, that remarkable boiling springs had been discovered on the sources of the Madison, by a party of trappers, in their spring hunt; of which the accounts they gave, were so very astonishing, that I determined to examine them myself, before recording their description, though I had the united testimony of more than twenty men on the subject, who all declared they saw them, and that they really were as extensive and remarkable as they had been described. Having now an opportunity of paying them a visit, and as another or a better might not occur,

[1] The narration was by a trapper for the American Fur Company, Warren A. Ferris, and his story first appeared in the *Western Literary Messenger* from July 13, 1842, until May 18, 1844. It has appeared in book form in recent years. See bibliography.

I parted with the company after supper, and taking with me two Pend d'Oreilles (who were induced to take the excursion with me by the promise of an extra present), set out at a round pace, the night being clear and comfortable. We proceeded over the plain about twenty miles, and halted until daylight, on a fine spring, flowing into Camas Creek. Refreshed by a few hours sleep, we started again after a hasty breakfast, and entered a very extensive forest, called the Pine Woods (a continued succession of low mountains or hills, entirely covered with a dense growth of this species of timber), which we passed through and reached the vicinity of the springs about dark, having seen several lakes or ponds on the sources of the Madison, and rode about forty miles; which was a hard day's ride, taking into consideration the rough irregularity of the country through which we traveled.

"We regaled ourselves with a cup of coffee, the materials for making which we had brought with us, and immediately after supper, lay down to rest, sleepy and much fatigued. The continual roaring of the springs, however, (which was distinctly heard) for some time prevented my going to sleep, and excited an impatient curiosity to examine them, which I was obliged to defer the gratification of until morning, and filled my slumbers with visions of waterspouts, cataracts, fountains, *jets d'eau* of immense dimensions, etc., etc.

"When I arose in the morning, clouds of vapor seemed like a dense fog to overhang the springs, from which frequent reports or explosions of different loudness, constantly assailed our ears. I immediately proceeded to inspect them, and might have exclaimed with the Queen of Sheba, when their full reality of dimensions and novelty burst upon my view, 'the half was not told me.'

"From the surface of a rocky plain or table burst forth columns of water of various dimensions, projecting high in the air, accompanied by loud explosions and sulphurous vapors, which were highly disagreeable to the smell. The rock from which these springs burst forth was calcareous, and probably extends some distance from them, beneath the soil. The larg-

42

HIRAM MARTIN CHITTENDEN

"For one man to be a good army officer, a top-drawer engineer, and a competent historian concurrently is an unusual phenomenon, and indeed, Hiram Martin Chittenden was a man of unusual and considerable talents."

CROW WARRIOR

"Physically, they were a stalwart, handsome race, fine horse-men and daring hunters."

BIRD RATTLER, CURLY BEAR, AND WOLF PLUME, BLACKFEET

"They were a tribe of perpetual fighters, justly characterized as the Ishmaelites of their race."

TUKUARIKA OR SHEEPEATER SHOSHONE

" . . . the only known aboriginal occupants of what is now the Yellowstone Park."

From E. S. Topping, *The Chronicles of the Yellowstone*

BANNOCK FAMILY

"The most important Indian trail in the Park, however, was that known as the Great Bannock Trail."

Yellowstone Library and Museum Association

JOHN COLTER'S RACE FOR LIFE

"Even this terrible adventure could not dismay the dauntless
Colter, and he remained still another year in the mountains."

From *Indian Anecdotes and Barbarities* (author unknown)

JIM BRIDGER

"He had explored and could accurately describe the wonders of the Yellowstone fully a quarter of a century before their final discovery."

CHIEF JOSEPH OF THE NEZ PERCÉS IN 1878

"He deservedly ranks among the most noted of the North American Indians. . . . No Indian Chief ever commanded to such a degree the respect and even friendship of his enemies."

est of these beautiful fountains projects a column of boiling water several feet in diameter to the height of more than one hundred and fifty feet, in my opinion; but the party of Alvarez, who discovered it, persist in declaring that it could not be less than four times that distance in height—accompanied with a tremendous noise. These explosions and discharges occur at intervals of about two hours. After having witnessed three of them, I ventured near enough to put my hand into the waters of its basin, but withdrew it instantly, for the heat of the water in this immense chaldron was altogether too great for my comfort; and the agitation of the water, the disagreeable effluvium continually exuding, and the hollow unearthly rumbling under the rock on which I stood, so ill accorded with my notions of personal safety, that I retreated back precipitately to a respectful distance. The Indians who were with me were quite appalled, and could not by any means be induced to approach them. They seemed astonished at my presumption in advancing up to the large one, and when I safely returned, congratulated me upon my 'narrow escape.' They believed them to be supernatural and supposed them to be the production of the Evil Spirit. One of them remarked that hell, of which he had heard from the whites, must be in that vicinity. The diameter of the basin into which the waters of the largest jet principally fall, and from the center of which, through a hole in the rock of about nine or ten feet in diameter, the water spouts up as above related, may be about thirty feet. There are many other smaller fountains that did not throw their waters up so high, but occurred at shorter intervals. In some instances the volumes were projected obliquely upward, and fell into the neighboring fountains, or on the rock or prairie. But their ascent was generally perpendicular, falling in and about their own basins or apertures.

"These wonderful productions of nature are situated near the center of a small valley, surrounded by pine-covered hills, through which a small fork of the Madison flows."

Here we have a description, as from the pen of some earlier Doane or Langford, free from exaggeration and true to the

43

facts. No one who has seen the Upper Geyser Basin will question its general correctness. The writer then goes on to relate what he has learned from others, but here exaggeration creeps in and this part of his narrative is less reliable. It continues:

"From several trappers who had recently returned from the Yellow Stone, I received an account of boiling springs that differ from those seen on Salt River only in magnitude, being on a vastly larger scale; some of their cones are from twenty to thirty feet high, and forty to fifty paces in circumference. Those which have ceased to emit boiling, vapor, etc., of which there were several, are full of shelving cavities, even some fathoms in extent, which give them, inside, an appearance of honey-comb. The ground for several acres extent in vicinity of the springs is evidently hollow, and constantly exhales a hot steam or vapor of disagreeable odor, and a character entirely to prevent vegetation. They are situated in the valley at the head of that river near the lake, which constitutes its source.

"A short distance from these springs, near the margin of the lake, there is one quite different from any yet described. It is of a circular form, several feet in diameter, clear, cold, and pure; the bottom appears visible to the eye, and seems seven or eight feet below the surface of the earth or water, without meeting any resistance. What is most singular with respect to this fountain is the fact that at regular intervals of about two minutes, a body or column of water bursts up to the height of eight feet, with an explosion as loud as the report of a musket, and then falls back into it; for a few seconds the water is roily, but it speedily settles and becomes transparent as before the effusion. A slight tremulous motion of the water, and a low rumbling sound from the caverns beneath, precede each explosion. This spring was believed to be connected with the lake by some subterranean passage, but the cause of its periodical eruptions or discharges is entirely unknown. I have never before heard of a cold spring whose waters exhibit the phenomena of periodical explosive propulsion in form of a jet. The geysers

44

of Iceland, and the various other European springs, the waters of which are projected upwards with violence and uniformity, as well as those seen on the head waters of the Madison, are invariably hot."

The cold water geyser above described, although apparently a myth, may not have been so after all. In many places along the west shore of the Yellowstone Lake there are visible protuberances in the water surface where boiling springs from beneath force the cold water upward. It is quite possible that this spring was so connected with the lake as to keep constantly filled with cold water to a considerable depth; and that the eruptive energy of the spring was expended in lifting the superincumbent mass without giving any visible indication of the thermal action below.

The whole article forms the most interesting and authentic reference to the geyser regions published prior to 1870. It proves beyond question that a knowledge of this region existed among the early trappers, and confirms our previous deduction that the wide range of the fur business could not have left it unexplored.

In a letter addressed by General Bonneville to the Montana Historical Society,* since the creation of the Yellowstone Park, he states that, at the time of his sojourn in the mountains, in 1831 34, the geyser regions were known to his men, although he had not personally seen them. He also remembered having seen the trader Alvarez, referred to in the above article.

In 1844, a large party of trappers entered the Upper Yellowstone Valley from the south, passed around the west shore of the Yellowstone Lake to the outlet, where they had a severe battle with the Blackfeet Indians in a broad open tract at that point. The remains of their old corral were still visible as late as 1870.

There are numerous other interesting, though less definite, references to an early knowledge of the Yellowstone; but those we have given show their general character. The important

* Montana Historical Society, *Transactions* (Helena. Rocky Mountain Publishing Co., 1876), Vol. I.

fact to remember is that this knowledge was barren of result. For the most part it existed only in the minds of illiterate men and perished with them. It never caught the public ear and did not in the least degree hasten the final discovery. Historically interesting these early adventures will always be, as are also the Norse voyages to America; but they are very far from being the Columbus voyage of discovery.

☆ 6 ☆

JAMES BRIDGER

OF THE EARLY CHARACTERS whose names are closely linked
with the history of the Yellowstone, the most distinguished is
James Bridger, a sketch of whose life is given in Appendix A,
under "Bridger Lake." That he had often been in the region
of the Yellowstone Park, and was familiar with its unique
features, is now well known. His first personal knowledge of
them is believed to date from 1824, when he is supposed to
have been upon the Upper Yellowstone. It is certain that before 1840 he knew of the existence of the geysers in the Firehole Valley, although at that time he had probably not seen
them himself. Between 1841 and 1844 Bridger was leader of
a grand hunting and trapping expedition, which for upward
of two years, wandered over the country from the Great Falls
of the Missouri to Chihuahua, Mexico. At some time during
this expedition he entered the region of the Upper Yellowstone
and saw most of its wonders. His descriptions of the geysers
and other remarkable features of that locality can be traced
back nearly to this period and present an accuracy of detail
which could come only from personal observation.[1]

Among the records of these descriptions the earliest is that
by Captain J. W. Gunnison, of the Corps of Topographical
Engineers, who was associated with Captain Howard Stans-
bury, of the same corps, in the Salt Lake Expedition of 1849–
50. The record is found in Gunnison's History of the Mormons,* and dates back to this expedition. It reads:

[1] See Appendix A, V, for a brief biography of Bridger.
* Captain J. W. Gunnison, *A History of the Mormons, or Latter Day
Saints* (Philadelphia, J. B. Lippincott & Co., 1856), 151.

47

"He [Bridger] gives a picture, most romantic and enticing, of the head waters of the Yellow Stone. A lake, sixty miles long, cold and pellucid, lies embosomed among high precipitous mountains. On the west side is a sloping plain, several miles wide, with clumps of trees and groves of pine. The ground resounds with the tread of horses. Geysers spout up seventy feet high with a terrific, hissing noise, at regular intervals. Waterfalls are sparkling, leaping, and thundering down the precipices and collect in the pool below. The river issues from this lake, and for fifteen miles roars through the perpendicular cañon at the outlet. In this section are the 'Great Springs,' so hot that meat is readily cooked in them, and as they descend on the successive terraces, afford at length delightful baths. On the other side is an acid spring, which gushes out in a river torrent; and below is a cave, which supplies 'vermillion' for the savages in abundance."

In this admirable summary we readily discover the Yellowstone Lake, the Grand Cañon, the Falls, the geyser basins, the Mammonth Hot Springs, and Cinnabar Mountain. Prior to 1860, Bridger had related these accounts to Captain Warren, Captain Raynolds, Doctor Hayden, and others, and although he seems to have convinced these gentlemen that there was something in his stories, they still attributed less to fact than to fancy.

In his efforts to disseminate a knowledge of this region, Bridger was as determined as Colter had been before him, and with little better success. He tried to have his narratives published, but no periodical would lend itself to his service. The editor of the *Kansas City Journal* stated editorially in 1879 that Bridger had told him of these wonders fully thirty years before. He prepared an article from Bridger's description, but suppressed it because his friends ridiculed the whole thing as incredible. He later publicly apologized to Bridger, who was then living at Westport, Missouri.*

* Of interest in this connection is the following extract from a recent letter to the writer by the present managing editor of the *Kansas City Journal:*
"The interview had with Bridger was in the year 1856. He told Col. R. T.

The persistent incredulity of his countrymen, and their ill-concealed suspicion of his honesty, to say nothing of his mental soundness, were long a cloud upon Bridger's life; but, more fortunate than his prototype, Colter, he lived to see himself triumphantly vindicated. Whether from disgust at this unmerited treatment, or because of his love of a good story, Bridger seems finally to have resolved that distrust of his word, if it must exist, should at least have some justification. He was in fact noted for "drawing the long bow to an unparalleled tension," and for never permitting troublesome scruples of conscience to interfere with the proper embellishment of his yarns. These were generally based upon fact, and diligent search will discover in them the "soul of truth" which, according to Herbert Spencer, always exists "in things erroneous." These anecdotes are current even yet among the inhabitants of the Yellowstone, and the tourist who remains long in the Park will not fail to hear them.

When Bridger found that he could not make his hearers believe in the existence of a vast mass of volcanic glass, now known to all tourists as the interesting Obsidian Cliff, he supplied them with another glass mountain of a truly original sort. Its discovery was the result of one of his hunting trips and it happened in this wise.

Coming one day in sight of a magnificent elk, he took careful aim at the unsuspecting animal and fired. To his great amazement, the elk not only was not wounded, but seemed not even to have heard the report of the rifle. Bridger drew considerably

Van Horn, Editor of the *Journal,* which was published at that time, the story of the Park with the geysers, and at the same time, drew with a piece of wrapping paper an outline of the route necessary to be taken by a railroad should it ever cross the continent, which route is exactly on the line that is now crossed by the Union Pacific.

"In this conversation, he told the Colonel about the mud springs and the other wonders of that part of the country, or to use his own expression, 'it was a place where hell bubbled up.'

"The Colonel was much interested in the matter at the time and took notes of the account, but did not print it because a man who claimed to know Bridger told him that he would be laughed out of town if he printed 'any of old Jim Bridger's lies.' "

nearer and gave the elk the benefit of his most deliberate aim, but with the same result as before. A third and a fourth effort met with a similar fate. Utterly exasperated, he seized his rifle by the barrel, resolved to use it as a club since it had failed as a firearm. He rushed madly toward the elk, but suddenly crashed into an immovable vertical wall which proved to be a mountain of perfectly transparent glass, on the farther side of which, still in peaceful security, the elk was quietly grazing. Stranger still, the mountain was not only of pure glass, but was a perfect telescopic lens, and, whereas, the elk seemed but a few hundred yards off, it was in reality twenty-five miles away!

Another of Bridger's discoveries was an ice-cold spring near the summit of a lofty mountain, the water from which flowed down over a long smooth slope, where it acquired such a velocity that it was boiling hot when it reached the bottom.*

An account, in which the "soul of truth" is not so readily apparent, is that of a mining prospector of this region, who, in later times, met a unique and horrible fate. He had for days been traveling with a party toward a prodigious diamond set in the top of a mountain, where, even at noonday, it shone with a luster surpassing the sun. He arrived at length on the top of the mountain only to see the diamond on another summit apparently as far away as ever. Disheartened and weary, he thought to save the labor of descent by taking advantage of an extremely smooth face of the mountain, and accordingly sat down upon his shovel, as upon a toboggan, and let slide. There was a vacant place around the camp-fire that evening,

* This story, which is taken from the report of Captain W. F. Raynolds, was one of Bridger's favorites, and it is even said that he did not regard it as pleasantry at all, but as plain matter of fact. Mr. Langford, who often heard him relate it, says that he generally described the stream as flowing over the smooth surface of a rock, and reasoned that, as two sticks rubbed together produce heat by friction, so the water rubbing over the rock became hot. In proof, he cited an instance where the water was hot only in close proximity to the rock and not at the surface. Mr. Langford found a partial confirmation of the fact, but not of the theory, in fording the Firehole River in 1870. He passed over the smooth deposit of an active hot spring in the bed of the stream and found that the stream bottom and the water in contact with it were hot.

and next day the rest of the party, passing along the base of the mountain, found an infusible clay pipe and the molten remains of a shovel. Warned by the fate of their comrade, the superstitious survivors forbore any further search for the diamond.

To those who have visited the west shore of the Yellowstone Lake and know how simple a matter it is to catch the lake trout and cook them in the boiling pools without taking them from the line, the ground work of the following description will be obvious enough. Somewhere along the shore an immense boiling spring discharges its overflow directly into the lake. The specific gravity of the water is less than that of the lake, owing probably to the expansive action of heat, and it floats in a stratum three or four feet thick upon the cold water underneath. When Bridger was in need of fish it was to this place that he went. Through the hot upper stratum he let fall his bait to the subjacent habitable zone, and having hooked his victim, cooked him *on the way out!*

In like manner the visitor to the region of petrifactions on Specimen Ridge in the north-east corner of the Park, and to various points in the hot springs districts, will have no difficulty in discovering the base material out of which Bridger contrived the following picturesque yarn. According to his account there exists in the Park country a mountain which was once cursed by a great medicine man of the Crow nation. Every thing upon the mountain at the time of this dire event became instantly petrified and has remained so ever since. All forms of life are standing about in stone where they were suddenly caught by the petrifying influences, even as the inhabitants of ancient Pompeii were surprised by the ashes of Vesuvius. Sage brush, grass, prairie fowl, antelope, elk, and bears may there be seen as perfect as in actual life. Even flowers are blooming in colors of crystal, and birds soar with wings spread in motionless flight, while the air floats with music and perfumes siliceous, and the sun and the moon shine with petrified light!

In this way Bridger avenged himself for the spirit of distrust so often shown for what he had related. The time presently came, however, when the public learned not only how large a measure of truth there was in his stories, but also how ingenious a tale he could weave from very inadequate material.

7

RAYNOLDS' EXPEDITION

ON THE 13th of April, 1859, Captain W. F. Raynolds, of the Corps of Topographical Engineers, U.S.A., was ordered to explore "the region of country through which flow the principal tributaries of the Yellowstone River, and the mountains in which they, and the Gallatin and Madison Forks of the Missouri, have their source." This was the first government expedition directly to the precise locality which is now embraced in the Yellowstone National Park.* It is interesting to us, not for what it accomplished—for it fortunately failed to penetrate the Upper Yellowstone country—but because it gives an admirable résumé, in the form of a report and a map, of the geographical knowledge of that country down to the date of actual discovery.

Captain Raynolds was in the field during the two seasons of 1859 and 1860, but it was only in the summer of 1860 that he directed his efforts toward the country in which we are particularly interested. In May of that year the expedition left its winter quarters at Deer Creek, Wyo., and marched to the junction of the Wind River and the Popo Agie where these streams unite under the name of Bighorn River. Here the party divided. One division under Captain Raynolds was to ascend the Wind River to its source and then cross to the head waters of the Yellowstone. This stream they were to follow down to

---

* Accompanying this expedition as geologist was Dr. F. V. Hayden, whose name is so intimately connected with the history of the Yellowstone Park. James Bridger was guide to the party.

the Great Bend, and then cross over to the Three Forks of the Missouri. The other party, under Lieutenant Maynadier, was to skirt the east and north flanks of the Absaroka Range and to join the first party at the Three Forks, if possible, not later than July 1.

Captain Raynolds was charged with other instructions than those mentioned in his order, which must be kept in mind in order properly to account for the final outcome of the expedition. A total eclipse of the sun was to occur on July 18th of that year, and its line of greatest occultation lay north of the British boundary. It was desired that Captain Raynolds should be present in that locality in time to observe the eclipse. This condition, rather than impassable mountains or unmelted snows, was the chief obstacle to a thorough exploration of the Upper Yellowstone.

The two parties separated May 24. Captain Raynolds, according to his program, kept up the Wind River Valley, and with much difficulty effected a crossing by way of Union Pass —which he named—to the western slope of the mountains. He then turned north seeking a passage to the head waters of the Yellowstone. When nearly opposite Two-Ocean Pass, he made a strenuous effort to force his way through, spending two days in the attempt. But it was still June and the snow lay deep on the mountains. It was a physical impossibility to get through at that point, and the risk of missing the eclipse forebade efforts elsewhere. The Captain was deeply disappointed at this result. He writes:

"My fondly cherished schemes of this nature were all dissipated by the prospect before us; . . . and I therefore very reluctantly decided to abandon the plan to which I had so steadily clung."

It seems not a little singular that so experienced a guide as Bridger should not have conducted the party up the valley of the Snake River and thence over the low divide between that stream and the Yellowstone Lake—a route which was perfectly practicable even as early as June. But the plan does not appear to have been entertained, and the expedition passed around the Park region to the west, arriving at the Three Forks on the twenty-ninth of June.

Lieutenant Maynadier wisely made no attempt to cross the Absaroka Range, which rose continuously on his left. Had he done so, the deep snow at that season would have rendered his efforts futile. He kept close to the flank of the mountains until he reached the valley of the Yellowstone north of the Park, and then hastened to join his commanding officer at the appointed rendezvous. He reached the Three Forks on the third day of July.

The expedition had now completely encircled the region of the Upper Yellowstone. At one point Captain Raynolds had stood where his eye could range over all that country which has since become so famous; but this was the limit of his endeavor. The Yellowstone wonderland was spared the misfortune of being discovered at so early a day—a fact quite as fortunate as any in its history.

It will be interesting now to survey this region as known at the time of the Raynolds Expedition. Nothing of importance occurred to increase public knowledge of it until 1870, and Captain Raynolds'* *Report* is therefore the latest authentic utterance concerning it prior to the date of actual discovery. In this report Captain Raynolds says:

"Beyond these [the mountains south-east of the Park], is the valley of the Upper Yellowstone, which is as yet a *terra incognita*. My expedition passed entirely around, but could not penetrate it. . . . Although it was June, the immense body of snow baffled all our exertions, and we were compelled to content ourselves with listening to marvelous tales of burning plains, immense lakes, and boiling springs, without being able to verify these wonders. I know of but two men who claim to have ever visited this part of the Yellowstone Valley—James Bridger and Robert Meldrum.[1] The narratives of both these

* Brevet General W. F. Raynolds, *Report of the Exploration of the Yellowstone and Missouri Rivers, in 1859–60* (Washington, Government Printing Office, 1868).

1 Robert Meldrum was a trapper who worked at one time for the American

men are very remarkable, and Bridger, in one of his recitals, described an immense boiling spring, that is a perfect counterpart of the geysers of Iceland. As he is uneducated, and had probably never heard of the existence of such natural wonders elsewhere, I have little doubt that he spoke of that which he had actually seen. . . . Bridger also insisted that immediately west* of the point at which we made our final effort to penetrate this singular valley, there is a stream of considerable size, which divides and flows down either side of the water-shed, thus discharging its waters into both the Atlantic and Pacific Oceans."

The Captain concludes this particular part of his report as follows:

"I can not doubt, therefore, that at no very distant day, the mysteries of this region will be fully revealed; and, although small in extent, I regard the valley of the Upper Yellowstone as the most interesting unexplored district in our widely expanded country."

Lieutenant Maynadier also contributes a few interesting observations upon this region. The vast importance of that extensive mass of mountains, as a reservoir of waters for the country round about, impressed him deeply. He says, somewhat ostentatiously:

"As my fancy warmed with the wealth of desolation before me, I found something to admire in the calm self-denial with which this region, content with barren magnificence, gives up its water and soil to more favored countries."

Of the Yellowstone River, he was told that it had its source "in a lake in the impenetrable fastnesses of the Rocky Mountains"; and that for some distance below the lake it flowed through a narrow gorge, up which "no one has even been able to travel."

But it is the map prepared by Captain Raynolds that tells a more interesting story even than his written report. It reveals

Fur Company. Washington Irving, *The Adventures of Captain Bonneville, U.S.A.* (ed. by Edgeley W. Todd), xxix–xxx.

* Actually north-east.

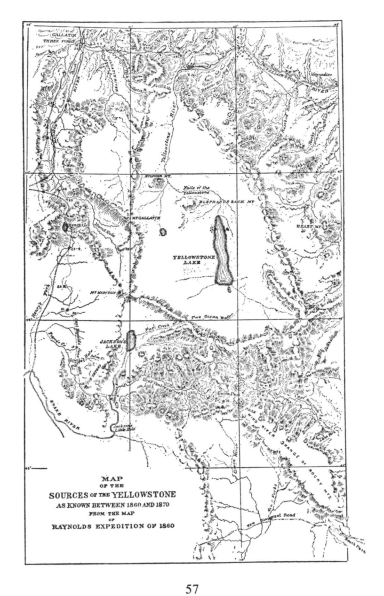

MAP
OF THE
SOURCES OF THE YELLOWSTONE
AS KNOWN BETWEEN 1860 AND 1870
FROM THE MAP
OF
RAYNOLDS EXPEDITION OF 1860

at once to the eye what was known as well as what was unknown of the Upper Yellowstone. Extending in a south-easterly and north-westerly direction, is a large elliptical space, within which geographical features are represented by dotted lines, indicating that they are put in by hearsay only. In the midst of a surrounding country, which is already mapped with great accuracy, there is a region wholly unknown to the geographer. A cordon of mountains encircles it and shows the limit of official effort to gain a correct knowledge of it. Within this enchanted enclosure lies the region approximately defined by the 44th and 45th parallels of latitude and the 110th and 111th meridians of longitude, which now constitutes the Yellowstone National Park. There one may catch glimpses, through the uncertain haze of tradition, of the geysers, hot springs, Lake, Falls, Grand Cañon, Mammoth Hot Springs, and Two-Ocean Pass. This was the net result of fifty years' desultory wandering in and about and over this "mystic" region.

Raynolds' report, it must be remembered, was the first official recognition in any form of the probable existence of extensive volcanic phenomena in the region of the Upper Yellowstone. Had it been published immediately after the expedition, and had not public attention been totally engrossed with other matters of overshadowing importance, this region must have become fully known in the early Sixties. But within a month after the return of Captain Raynolds to civilization there had taken place the national election which was the signal for attempted armed disruption of the Union. A year later found every officer of the Army called to new fields of duty. Western exploration entirely ceased until 1865, and was not vigorously resumed for some years thereafter. Captain Raynolds' report did not appear until 1868, although his map was published several years earlier in order to meet a demand for it by the new settlers in western Montana. Nothing transpired in the meantime to make the general public familiar with this region, and the picture . . . given is . . . substantially correct down to the date of the celebrated Washburn expedition.

58

☆ 8 ☆

GOLD IN MONTANA

PERHAPS THE MOST FASCINATING pages of American history are those which recount the annals of the discoveries of gold and silver. No one can appreciate the magnitude of those various movements by a simple perusal of statistics of the mineral wealth which they disclosed. He must pass through the mining belts and note how almost every rod of ground, over vast tracts of country, is filled with prospect holes that attest the miner's former presence. If the trapper carried the tools of his trade to haunts remote and inaccessible, the miner, with his pick and shovel, certainly outdid him. One can readily understand that, as soon as such a movement should be directed toward the region of the Upper Yellowstone, the wonders of that region would speedily be revealed.

The presence of gold in the mountains of Montana was first noticed as far back as 1852. Later, in 1858, the Stuart brothers, James and Granville, founders of Montana, discovered gold in the Deer Lodge Valley; but they were destitute of equipments and so constantly exposed to the hostility of the Blackfeet that they went to Fort Bridger in the south-west corner of Wyoming, and did not return until late in 1860.

It was in 1860 and 1861 that the rich mines on the Salmon and Boisé rivers were discovered. In 1862 the tide of discovery swept across the mountains into Montana. The rich mines on Pioneer Creek, the Big Prickly Pear, the Big Hole River, North Boulder Creek, and at Bannock and other points, became known. Although there were scarcely a thousand people in Montana in the winter of 1862–63, the news of the great discoveries marshaled a host of immigrants ready to enter the territory in the following spring. These were largely re-enforced by adventurers from both the northern and southern states, who, with little credit to their courage or patriotism, sought in these remote regions exemption from the tributes and levies of war. The immigrants were welcomed in the spring of 1863 by the news of the discovery of Alder Gulch, the richest of all gold placers. The work of prospecting, already being pushed with vigor, was stimulated to an extraordinary degree by this magnificent discovery. Prospecting parties scoured the country in all directions, often with loss of life through the Indians, but rarely, after the first two or three years, with any substantial success. Some of these expeditions have a particular connection with our narrative because they passed across portions of what is now the Yellowstone Park.

The most important of them occurred in August and September, 1863. It was led by Walter W. DeLacy, an engineer and surveyor of some distinction in the early history of Montana. The party at one time numbered forty-two men, although this number did not continue constant throughout the expedition. Its sole object was to "prospect" the country. Evidently nothing in the line of topographical reconnaissance was thought of, for Captain DeLacy says "there was not a telescope, and hardly a watch, in the whole party."

The expedition left Virginia City August 3, passed south into Idaho until it struck the Snake River, and then ascended that stream to the region about Jackson Lake. Near the mouth of Buffalo Fork a halt was made, a corral was built to hold the stock, and a miners' meeting held at which rules were adopted to govern the miners in the contemplated examination of the country. The party then broke up into small groups and set out in different directions so as to cover as much ground as possible. The last four days of August were spent in this search, but with failure in every direction. This discouragement led to the abandonment of the expedition. Fifteen men set out for home by the way they had come, while DeLacy and twenty-seven men resolved to reach the Madison River and the settlements by going north. A day later this party entered the territory which is now the Yellowstone Park.

The route lay up the Snake River to its junction with Lewis River where the hot springs of that locality were discovered. Here another separation occurred. About half the party went back down the river to re-examine a locality where they thought they had found some fair prospects. They soon returned, however, unsuccessful. The main party under DeLacy ascended the hills to the west of the river to seek a more practicable route. They soon reached the summit of the plateau where they discovered what are now Hering and Beula lakes, and noted their divergent drainage. Thence they passed north over Pitchstone Plateau until they struck the valley of Moose Creek. They descended this stream for a few miles and came to a large lake, which they supposed to be tributary to either the Madison or the Yellowstone rivers. To their great surprise they found, upon rounding its southern point, that it drained *south* into the Snake. This is what is now called Shoshone Lake.

From the outlet of the lake, DeLacy sent a man down stream to examine the river. This reconnaissance resulted in the discovery of Lewis Lake and the hot springs basin there. When DeLacy resumed his route, he followed along the east shore of the lake to its northern extremity, and then ascended the beautiful open valley of DeLacy Creek. He crossed the Continental Divide at the head of the valley, and camped on the evening of September 8 some miles beyond the Divide toward the Firehole River. The next morning, September 9, 1863, he came upon the considerable stream of hot water which flows down a mountain ravine into the Lower Geyser Basin close by the Great Fountain Geyser. The reader will learn with some amazement that our party thought little enough of this wonderful locality to pass directly through it without halt or perceptible delay. Before the camping hour of the afternoon had arrived, they were many miles away at the junction of the Gibbon and Firehole rivers.

The other section of the party, which had gone down the Snake from its junction with Lewis River, soon returned, followed up the river to Lewis and Shoshone lakes, passed around the western end of the latter lake discovering its extensive geyser basin, and thence crossed over to the Madison. This stream they descended through the geyser basins, and followed the main party to the settlements.

DeLacy might have passed into history as the real discoverer of the Yellowstone wonderland, but for the fact that he failed to appreciate the true importance of what he saw. In that, however, he was no exception to the general rule of immigrants. The search for gold with them so far overshadowed all other matters that it would have required something more than geysers to divert them, even momentarily, from its prosecution. Although DeLacy kept a daily journal of his expedition and noted therein the various items of interest along his route, he did not publish it until 1876, long after public interest had been strongly attracted to the geyser regions. He did, however, publish a map of the country through which he passed, and on this map he correctly noted the drainage of Shoshone Lake —something which the Folsom, Washburn, and Hayden (1871), expeditions all failed to do. He also noted the various hot springs localities through which the party passed. In a letter published in Raymond's *Mineral Resources of the States and Territories West of the Rocky Mountains,* in 1869, before the date of the Washburn Expedition, he called attention to the existence of geysers at the head of Shoshone Lake and on the Madison River.

DeLacy's account, as finally published, is an interesting early view of this region, and is remarkable for its general correctness. That he failed to publish his discoveries must be regarded as fortunate so far as the Park is concerned, for the time had not yet come when it was desirable that the real character of this country should be made known.

From 1863 to 1869 there were many other prospecting parties in the region of the Upper Yellowstone. In 1863 one of these parties, numbering thirty or forty men, ascended the Yellowstone and the East Fork to the mouth of Soda Butte Creek, and thence crossed an intervening ridge to the next northern tributary of the East Fork. Here all their horses were stolen by Indians. There were left only one or two mules on which was packed all the baggage they could carry, the rest being concealed in a cache. The party then separated into two portions and prospected the country for several days in the vicinity of Clark's Fork. They finally returned, emptied the cache, and descended to the Yellowstone where they found fair prospects near the present north boundary of the Park. The expedition has no permanent interest for this narrative except that it left the two geographical names, "Cache Creek" and "Bear Gulch."

In 1864, a party of seventy-three men under James Stuart passed from Deer Lodge, Montana, to the Yellowstone Valley, and thence around the east base of the Absaroka Range into the valley of the Stinkingwater. The object of this expedition was to punish the Indians for outrages of the previous year, and also to prospect the country for gold. At the Stinkingwater, Stuart was compelled to return home. The party then separated into groups that gradually worked their way back to the Montana settlements. One of these small parties went as far south as the Sweetwater River, then crossed to the Green and Snake rivers, and recrossed the Continental Divide at Two-Ocean Pass. They descended the Yellowstone, past the Lake and Grand Cañon, and beyond the present limits of the Park. Norris found remnants of their camp debris seventeen years afterward.

In 1866, a party under one George Huston left Virginia City, Montana, and ascended the Madison River to the geyser basins. Thence they crossed to the Yellowstone at Mud Geyser, ascended the river to the lake, passed completely around the latter, discovering Hart Lake on their way, and then descended the Yellowstone by the Falls and Cañon, to Emigrant Gulch. Here they were interviewed by a newspaper reporter, and an account of their travels was published in the *Omaha Herald*. They had seen about all there was to be seen in the whole region.

At least two parties traversed the Park country in 1867.

One of these gave names to Crevice, Hell Roaring, and Slough creeks. An account of the wanderings of the other party appeared in the *Montana Post* of that year.

Many other parties and individuals passed through this region during the Montana mining craze. Their accounts appeared now and then in the local papers, and were reprinted throughout the country. By 1869, probably very few of the reading public had not heard rumors of a strange volcanic region in the Far West. In Montana, particularly, repeated confirmation of the old trappers' tales was gradually arousing a deep interest, and the time was fast approaching when explorations for the specific purpose of verifying these rumors were to begin.

☆ **9** ☆

DISCOVERY

THE DISCOVERY of the Yellowstone wonderland—by which is here meant its full and final disclosure to the world—was the work of three parties who visited and explored it in the years 1869, 1870, and 1871, respectively. The first of these expeditions was purely a private enterprise. It consisted of three men, and was the first party to enter this country with the express purpose of verifying or refuting the floating rumors concerning it. The second expedition was of a mixed character, having semi-official sanction, but being organized and recruited by private individuals. This was the famous "Yellowstone Expedition of 1870"—the great starting point in the post-traditional history of the Park. The third expedition was strictly official, under the military and scientific departments of the government. It was a direct result of the explorations of 1870 and was intended to satisfy the public demand for accurate and official information concerning this new region of wonders. It was the final and necessary step in order that the government might act intelligently and promptly for the preservation of what was believed to be the most interesting collection of wonders to be found in the world.*

THE EXPEDITION OF 1869

The question of setting definitely at rest the constantly multiplying rumors of wonderful volcanic phenomena around the sources of the Yellowstone began to be seriously agitated

* For diagram of routes, see Historical Chart, p. 13.

among the people of Montana as early as 1867. An expedition was planned for that year but came to nothing. A like result attended a similar effort the following year. In 1869, the proposition came near materializing but fell through at the last moment owing to the failure to obtain a military escort. There were three members of this proposed expedition, however, who refused to be frightened off by any dangers which the situation at that time promised. They had already provided themselves with an elaborate equipment, and were determined, with escort or without it, to undertake the trip. The names of these men were David E. Folsom, C. W. Cook, and William Peterson, the last named being a native of Denmark. Armed with "repeating rifles, Colt's six-shooters, and sheath-knives," with a "double-barreled shot gun for small game," and equipped with a "good field-glass, pocket compass and thermometer," and utensils and provisions "for a six weeks' trip," they set out from Diamond City on the Missouri River, forty miles from Helena, September 6, 1869.

The route lay up the Missouri to the Three Forks; thence via Bozeman and Fort Ellis to the Yellowstone River; and thence up the Yellowstone to its junction with the East Fork[1] inside the present limits of the Park. From this point they crossed to the east bank and followed up the river, passing through the many groups of hot springs to be found east of the Grand Cañon. On September 21, they arrived at the Falls of the Yellowstone, where they remained an entire day. Some distance above the rapids they re-crossed to the west shore and then ascended the river past Sulphur Mountain and Mud Volcano to Yellowstone Lake. They then went to the extreme west shore of the lake and spent some time examining the surpassingly beautiful springs at that point. Thence they crossed the mountains to Shoshone Lake, which they took to be the head of the Madison, and from that point struck out to the northwest over a toilsome country until they reached the Lower Geyser Basin near Nez Percé Creek. Here they saw the Foun-

[1] Now known as Lamar Creek.

66

tain Geyser in action and the many other phenomena in that locality. They ascended the Firehole River to Excelsior Geyser and Prismatic Lake, and then turned down the river on their way home. They were absent on the expedition thirty-six days.

It is said that these explorers were so astonished at the marvels they had seen that "they were, on their return, unwilling to risk their reputations for veracity by a full recital of them to a small company whom their friends had assembled to hear the account of their explorations." But Mr. Folsom later prepared a most entertaining narrative of his journey which was published in the *Western Monthly,* of Chicago, in July, 1871. This article deserves a high rank in the literature of the Park. It is free from exaggeration and contains some descriptions unsurpassed by any subsequent writer. The article, and personal interviews with the author and his companions, had a strong influence in leading to the important expedition next to be described.

THE EXPEDITION OF 1870

The Yellowstone Expedition of 1870, more commonly known at the Washburn-Doane Expedition, was the culmination of the project of discovery to which frequent reference has already been made. At this time the subject was exciting a profound interest throughout Montana, and the leading citizens of the territory were active in organizing a grand expedition. General Sheridan, who passed through Helena just prior to his departure for the scene of the Franco-German War, spent some time in arranging for a military escort to accompany the party. The project did not assume definite shape until about the middle of August, and when the time for departure arrived, Indian alarms caused a majority of the party to repent their decision to join it. Finally, there were only nine persons who were willing to brave all dangers for the success of the undertaking. These nine were:

General Henry D. Washburn, Surveyor-General of Montana, chief of the expedition, and author of a series of valuable "notes" describing it.[2]

Hon. Nathaniel P. Langford, who published a series of articles in *Scribner's Magazine,** which gave general publicity to the news of discovery. He became first superintendent of the Park.

Hon. Cornelius Hedges, who first proposed setting apart this region as a national park.

Hon. Truman C. Everts, ex-U.S. assessor for Montana, whose experience upon the expedition forms the most painful and thrilling chapter in the annals of the Yellowstone.

Hon. Samuel T. Hauser, president of the First National Bank of Helena, and later governor of Montana.

Walter Trumbull, son of the late Senator Trumbull. He published an account of the expedition in the *Overland Monthly* for June, 1871.

Other civilian members of the expedition were Benjamin Stickney, Jr., Warren C. Gillette, and Jacob Smith.

The personnel of this party is sufficient evidence of the widespread interest which was being taken at the time in the region of the Upper Yellowstone.

The party proceeded from Helena to Fort Ellis, one hundred and twenty-five miles, where they were to receive a military escort promised by General Hancock, at that time commanding the department in which Fort Ellis was located. The post order detailing this escort is dated August 21, 1870, and directs Lieutenant Gustavus C. Doane, Second Cavalry, with one sergeant and four privates, "to escort the Surveyor-General of Montana to the falls and lakes of the Yellowstone and return." There is a significant absence in this order of any reference to geysers or hot springs; and the discreet post commander

2 In his bibliography, Chittenden listed under the heading of "Yellowstone Expedition of 1870" a series of "notes," not only by General Washburn, but also by N. P. Langford and Cornelius Hedges, which appeared in the *Helena Herald* and the *Helena Gazette* between September 26, 1870, and November 12, 1870.

* "The Wonders of the Yellowstone," Vol. II, No. 1 (May, 1871), 1–17; Vol. II, No. 2 (June, 1871), 113–28.

evidently did not intend to commit himself to a recognition of their existence on the strength of such knowledge as was then available. His incredulity was indeed largely shared by the members of the party themselves. Mr. Hedges subsequently said:

"I think a more confirmed set of sceptics never went out into the wilderness than those who composed our party, and never was a party more completely surprised and captivated with the wonders of nature."

Lieutenant Doane, than whom no member of the expedition holds a more honorable place in its history, has left on record a similar confession.

The party as finally organized, including two packers and two colored cooks, numbered nineteen individuals. Thirty-five horses and mules, thoroughly equipped for a month's absence, completed the "outfit," and made altogether quite an imposing cavalcade.

August 22, 1870, the expedition left Fort Ellis, crossed to the Yellowstone, and ascended that stream through the First and Second Cañons, past the "Devil's Slide" and Cinnabar Mountain, to the present north boundary line of the Park at the mouth of the Gardiner River. At this point they were within five miles of the celebrated Mammoth Hot Springs which are now the first attraction to meet the tourist's eye on entering the Park. But the party kept close to the Yellowstone, instead of taking the modern route up the Gardiner, and missed this wonder altogether.

It was August 26 when the expedition entered the present territory of the Park. Lieutenant Doane and Mr. Everts, with one soldier and two hunters picked up on the way, rode in advance along the brink of the Third Cañon and across the high plateau between the Gardiner and Tower Creek, camping at nightfall upon the latter stream. In the broad open valley near the junction of the Yellowstone and East Fork, a small tepid sulphur spring gave them the first evidence of their approach to the regions of volcanic activity.

Next day, the remainder of the party arrived. Two days

were spent in examining the beautiful Tower Falls, and—to our tyros in geyser exploration—the wonderful hot spring formations to be seen at that point. Here they also had for the first time glimpses of the Grand Cañon of the Yellowstone.

The party left Tower Creek on the twenty-ninth of August, and followed up the river over the east flank of Mount Washburn. As their progress lifted them rapidly above the surrounding country, a marvelously beautiful landscape unfolded itself to their view. Presently an interesting incident occurred, which shall stand here in Lieutenant Doane's own language:

"Through the mountain gap formed by the cañon, and on the interior slopes some twenty [evidently a misprint] miles distant, an object now appeared which drew a simultaneous expression of wonder from every one of the party. A column of steam, rising from the dense woods to the height of several hundred feet, became distinctly visible. We had all heard fabulous stories of this region, and were somewhat skeptical of appearances. At first it was pronounced a fire in the woods, but presently some one noticed that the vapor rose in regular puffs, as if expelled with great force. Then conviction was forced upon us. It was indeed a great column of steam, puffing away on the lofty mountain side, escaping with a roaring sound audible at a long distance, even through the heavy forest. A hearty cheer rang out at this discovery, and we pressed onward with renewed enthusiasm."

The party then ascended the lofty mountain to their right, now known as Mt. Washburn, and from its summit looked around upon the vast panorama which is now included in the Yellowstone National Park. Had old James Bridger been present at that moment he would have received ample vindication for long-standing injustice at the hands of his incredulous countrymen. *There* were the Cañon and Falls and Lake of the Yellowstone, with evidence enough of boiling springs and geysers! The enthusiasm of the party was unbounded, and Lieutenant Doane exultingly declares that they were "more than satisfied with the opening up of the campaign."

The pack-train continued its course along the side of the mountain and went into camp after a march of only twelve miles. That evening, Messrs. Washburn, Doane, and Hedges went on ahead of the main party, discovering the extensive mud springs at the southern base of the mountain, and finally reached the verge of a cliff beyond which yawned the stupendous cañon of the Yellowstone. It was the first real view from near by, but darkness prevented further examination.

The next day saw the arrival of the party at the Falls of the Yellowstone, close by the mouth of Cascade Creek, which, with its Crystal Falls, received that day their present names. The remainder of this day, August 30, and the next, were spent in exploring the cañon and measuring the heights of the falls. Messrs. Hauser and Stickney descended the sides of the cañon to the brink of the river about two miles below the falls; and Lieutenant Doane and Private McConnell accomplished the same difficult feat further down. It needs not to be said that the members of the party were profoundly impressed with the incomparable scenery of the Grand Cañon, although their descriptions of it are, perhaps, least satisfactory of any they have left us.

From the Cañon the party ascended the now placid river amid ever-changing wonders. They passed Sulphur Mountain and the uncanny region around the Mud Volcano and Mud Geyser, then crossed to the east shore of the river, and finally went into camp, September 3, on the shore of the Yellowstone Lake. Here our explorers were again in ecstasies, and not without cause; for, seen under favoring conditions, this "watery solitude" is one of the most beautiful objects in nature.

After a day spent in this camp, the expedition continued by slow stages up the east shore of the lake. Messrs. Doane and Langford scaled the lofty Absaroka Range just east of the lake, being the first white men known to have accomplished this feat, and their names now designate two of its noblest summits.

September 7 the party forded the Upper Yellowstone and traversed the almost impassable labyrinths of fallen timber between the several projecting arms on the south of the lake. It was on this portion of the route, September 9, that Mr. Everts became separated from his party, lost his horse with all his accouterments, and commenced those "thirty-seven days of peril," which so nearly cost him his life. This unfortunate affair cast a deep gloom over the little party and seriously interfered with the progress of the expedition. A week was spent in searching for the lost companion, without other result than the discovery of the hot springs basins at Hart Lake and on the west shore of the Yellowstone Lake.

At length it was concluded that Mr. Everts had either been killed or had wandered back home, and it was resolved to wait no longer. The party were surfeited with sight-seeing, and believed that they had now covered the whole ground. They therefore determined to strike across the mountains to the Madison and follow that stream to the settlements. They set out on the morning of September 17, over rugged hills and through fallen timber, crossing the Continental Divide twice, and camping that night in an open glade on a small branch of the Firehole. While passing the second time over the Divide, they caught a glimpse of Shoshone Lake and erroneously thought it to be the head of the Firehole River.

At 9 A.M., September 18, the march was resumed. The party soon reached the Firehole just above Kepler Cascade and thence followed down the course of the stream. Tourists who have visited the Park since 1891, when the new road from the Upper Basin to the Lake was opened, will remember that immediately after leaving "Old Faithful" they plunge into an unbroken pine forest and see no other evidences of geyser action until they reach the Lake. The situation of our homeward-bound explorers can thus be easily understood. They were traveling toward the geysers. The dense forest concealed everything beyond the radius of a few hundred feet. In unsuspecting mood, bent only on getting home to tell their wonderful story, and perhaps to find their missing companion, they moved down the river, crossing it considerably below the site of the present bridge above the Upper Basin, and suddenly emerged from the timber into an open treeless valley. It was nearly noon of a clear, cool September day. Directly in front of them, scarcely two hundred yards away, a vertical column of water and steam was shooting upward a hundred and fifty feet into the air. The bright sunlight turned the clear water into a mass of glittering crystals, and a gentle breeze wafted the vast white curtain of steam far to the right across the valley. Thus it was that "Old Faithful," as if forewarned of the approach of her distinguished visitors, gave them her most graceful salutation; and thus she bowed out the era of tradition and fable, and ushered the civilized world into the untrodden empire of the Fire King. Little wonder that our astonished explorers "spurred their jaded horses" and "gathered around the wonderful phenomenon."

The party spent only the remainder of the day and the following morning in the Upper Basin, but in that time saw seven of the principal geysers in action and gave them their present names. They then passed down the river through the Middle and Lower basins, but stopped to examine only such curiosities as were close by the river. Their rations were nearly gone, their lost companion was not found, and the desire to tell what they had already seen was greater than the desire to see more.[3] They therefore made haste for home, and on the evening of September 19 encamped where the Firehole and Gibbon rivers unite to form the Madison. From this point the party journeyed steadily homeward, conversing on the expedition of the past month and planning how their great discovery might best be brought to the attention of the world.[4]

The news of this expedition created intense and wide-spread interest throughout the country. Messrs. Washburn, Hedges, Trumbull, and others, prepared numerous descriptive articles for the local Montana papers, many of them among the best that have ever been written upon the Park, and these were reproduced in every important paper in the land. The *Helena*

[3] Everts was rescued by a search party which found him close to the present northern boundary of the Park.

[4] It was here that Cornelius Hedges proposed the creation of a national park.

Herald of October 27, 1870, only a month after the return of the party, refers to the extraordinary interest aroused by these articles, so unlike the sixty years' indifference which had marked the history of this region.

These preliminary and hasty reports were followed by more studied efforts. Lieutenant Doane's masterly report was completed December 15, 1870. Besides its intrinsic merit, it has the distinction of being the first official report upon the Upper Yellowstone country. It passed through the customary military channels and was finally sent to Congress, February 24, 1871. Prof. S. F. Baird, of the Smithsonian Institution, also presented the information gathered by Lieutenant Doane to the Philosophical Society of Washington during the winter.

Messrs. Langford and Trumbull prepared entertaining magazine articles, which, however, could not be gotten to press until the following May and June. But Mr. Langford in the meantime did effective work from the lecture stand. In Helena, Minneapolis, New York and Washington, he told the story of what he had seen. In Washington, the Hon. James G. Blaine, speaker of the House, presided at the lecture, and in the audience was Dr. F. V. Hayden, who was destined to play a prominent part in the history of the Yellowstone Park.

From whatever point of view considered, this expedition is one of the most remarkable in our annals. From Helena to the farthest point reached by the party, the route passed over was nearly three hundred miles long. The region of the Upper Yellowstone is perhaps the most difficult of access in the entire country. Even to-day, it is an almost certain place in which to get lost, if one is not thoroughly familiar with wilderness travel and happens to stray away from the beaten path. In 1870, moreover, the danger from hostile Indians was a constant and formidable menace, and the party was more than once reminded of it during the progress of the expedition. But in spite of all these difficulties, the success of the enterprise was so complete, its incidents were so full of romance, and its results were so far-reaching and important, that it well deserves the wide attention it has received.

THE JOINT GOVERNMENT EXPEDITION OF 1871

The direct result of the expedition of 1870 was to cause the U.S. Geological Survey[5] to change its program for the season of 1871, so as to give attention to the new wonderland, and also to cause the military authorities to send a well-appointed engineer party to the same locality. These two expeditions, one under Dr. Hayden and the other under Captains Barlow and Heap, of the Engineer Corps of the Army, moved for the most part together, camping near each other, and accompanied by the same military escort. Particular attention will here be given only to such features of these expeditions as pertain to new discoveries.

At the very outset of their journey, they branched off from the Washburn route at the mouth of the Gardiner River, and by ascending this stream, discovered the wonderful formations now known as the Mammoth Hot Springs. From this point, the parties traveled eastward to Tower Creek; thence over Mt. Washburn, and past the Cañon and Falls, to Sulphur Mountain, Mud Geyser, and the Lake; thence by a new route across the mountains to the Lower Geyser Basin; thence to the Upper Basin; thence east, across the mountains again, past Shoshone Lake to Yellowstone Lake; thence around the head of this body of water to its outlet; thence across the country, by separate routes, to the mouth of Soda Butte Creek; and thence down the East Fork to Baronett's Bridge[6] (which had been built only a few months before), and out of the Park by way of Mammoth Hot Springs.

The original work done by these parties, besides the discovery of the springs on the Gardiner, was the opening of a route between the Yellowstone River and the Lower Geyser Basin, the exploration of the Lower Basin, the mapping of the shore line of Yellowstone Lake by Dr. Hayden, the mapping

5 This is the U.S. Geological and Geographical Survey of the Territories, F. V. Hayden, Geologist in Charge. The present U.S. Geological Survey was created in 1879.

6 Baronett's bridge was at the junction of Lamar Creek (here called the East Fork) with the Yellowstone.

of the head waters of the Snake River by Captain Barlow, and some hasty explorations in the valley of the East Fork of the Yellowstone, now called Lamar River.

The chief value of these explorations, however, was not in the line of original discovery, but in the large collection of accurate data concerning the entire region. The photographs were of immense value. Description might exaggerate, but the camera told the truth; and in this case the truth was more remarkable than exaggeration. Unfortunately for Captain Barlow's collection, the great Chicago fire almost entirely destroyed it. The same cause delayed the appearance of his report until six weeks after the Park Bill was passed. An interesting and complete summary, however, appeared as a supplement in the *Chicago Journal* for January 13, 1872. The report and collection of photographs and specimens by Dr. Hayden were therefore the principal results of this season's work, and they played a decisive part in the events of the winter of 1871–72.

With the close of the expeditions of 1871, the discovery of the Yellowstone wonderland was made complete. It remained to see what Congress would do with so unique and valuable a possession.

☆ 10 ☆

THE NATIONAL PARK IDEA
—ITS ORIGIN AND REALIZATION

THE FIRST STEAMBOAT to ascend the Missouri River as far as to the mouth of the Yellowstone arrived at that point on the twenty-sixth of June, 1832. By a happy coincidence it bore the name *Yellowstone*. We are indebted for the conception of the National Park idea to a passenger upon this boat who was destined to become one of the most interesting characters America has produced. Every one bears in memory those pictures of Indian life which thrilled their youthful imagination with visions of camping-grounds, council fires, exciting buffalo hunts, and the wild and picturesque costumes of the red men. Very few, however, realize how largely all that is best in these pictures has flowed from a single source. The name of George Catlin is by no means familiar except to the specialist. His work reaches the public eye through so many different channels, and so often without any acknowledgment of its origin, that the origin itself is very generally lost to view.

To no other individual does the Indian race owe so much for the perpetuity in history and art of its life and customs. From an early age he displayed an enthusiasm for every thing pertaining to the aboriginal races which can be adequately described only by the word worship. He abandoned the profession for which he had been educated and enlisted his whole energy in the service of brush and pencil, apparently for the single purpose of indulging this passion of his life. He once wrote:

"Unaided and unadvised, I resolved to use my art and so much of the labors of my future life as might be required in

77

rescuing from oblivion the looks and customs of the vanishing races of native man in America, to which I plainly saw they were hastening before the approach and certain progress of civilization."

This high purpose Catlin followed throughout the remainder of his life with unwavering fidelity. He visited almost every Indian tribe in North America, gathering sketches and making descriptive notes. He also visited South America, and afterward spent many years in Europe exhibiting his work. The result of his labors was a gallery of more than six hundred pictures, now happily forever safe under the protection of the Smithsonian Institution in Washington, wherein he delineated the portraits of famous chiefs and the scenes and customs of Indian life. This work he supplemented with the scarcely less valuable work of his pen, leaving behind him probably the best popular description of the native races that has ever been written. His work is a perennial fountain to which students of Indian themes will ever resort. Valuable as it was considered in his lifetime, each passing year makes it more valuable still.

Catlin's enthusiasm for every thing pertaining to Indian life and the grief with which he beheld the certain fading away of it all before the rapid progress of civilization, suggested to him the idea which was to find partial fulfillment at the time to which our narrative has now been carried. In order to preserve, at least on a small scale, the native fauna of America and a remnant of the Indian races, he proposed that the government should set apart, in some suitable locality of the West, a large tract of land, to be preserved forever as a *"Nation's Park,* containing man and beast, in all the wildness and freshness of their nature's beauty." With his natural enthusiasm and vigor, he unfolded his idea, concluding:

"I would ask no other monument to my memory, nor any other enrollment of my name among the famous dead, than the reputation of having been the founder of such an institution."[1]

[1] George Catlin, *North American Indians,* I, 294–95. There are many editions, and the page numbers will vary considerably.

In the report of the late Prof. Joseph Henry to the Board of Regents of the Smithsonian Institution for 1871, it is stated that Catlin made a proposition to the government in 1832 "to reserve the country around these [the Yellowstone] geysers as a public park."[2] While it is more than probable, considering the date, and the wide acquaintance of Mr. Catlin with the traders and Indians of the West, that he had heard of the geyser regions, still there is not sufficient evidence attainable to justify our acceptance of the above statement. But in everything else except the particular locality, and the plan of providing a reservation for the Indians, Catlin's idea was the same as that finally adopted by Congress.

Although the project of creating a vast national park in the West originated with George Catlin, it is certain that Congress could never have been brought to act favorably upon it, except under the influence of some extraordinary motive. That motive was supplied when the innumerable unique and marvelous wonders of the Yellowstone were made known. Their preservation at once became a matter of high public duty, which could be accomplished only by reserving from settlement the region around them.

Since the Park was created and has to such a marked degree received the approval of the people, numerous claimants have arisen for the honor of having first suggested the idea. In truth, no special credit for originality should attach to the matter. It was a natural, an unavoidable proposition. To those who first saw these wonders, and were not so absorbed with gold-seeking as to be incapable of appreciating their importance, it was clear that, within a few years, they must become objects of universal interest. It was equally clear that the land around them would soon be taken up by private parties, and that the beautiful formations would be carried off for mercenary purposes; in short, that the history of Niagara and of the Yosemite would repeat itself in the Yellowstone. To avoid such a calamity only one course was open, and that was for the government to retain control of the entire region. That the necessity of such a course

2 Departmental Edition, 28.

should have been set forth independently by several different parties, as we find it to have been, is therefore not in the least surprising.

But in as much as the development of the project must have started from some one source, it is of interest historically to determine what this source was. We find it to have been the Washburn Expedition of 1870.* The subject was discussed by the party at the first camp after leaving the geyser regions near the junction of the Firehole and Gibbon rivers. The date was September 19, 1870. The members of the party were sitting around the camp-fire after supper, conversing about what they had seen and picturing to themselves the important pleasure resort which so wonderful a region must soon become. The natural impulse to turn the fruits of discovery to the personal profit of the discoverer made its appearance, and it was suggested that it would be a "profitable speculation" to take up land around the various objects of interest. The conversation had not proceeded far on these lines when one of the party, Cornelius Hedges, interposed and said that private ownership of that region, or any part of it, ought never to be countenanced, but that it ought to be set apart by the government and forever held to the unrestricted use of the people. This higher view of the subject found immediate acceptance with the other members of the party. It was agreed that the project should be at once set afoot and pushed vigorously to a finish.

As soon as the party reached Helena, a series of articles appeared in the daily papers of that city describing the late expedition, and in one of these, written by Mr. Hedges and published in the *Helena Herald* November 9, 1870, occurs what is believed to be the first public reference to the Park project.

* Mr. Folsom deserves mention in this connection. In the manuscript of his article in the *Western Monthly* was a reference to the Park idea; but the publishers cut out a large part of his paper, giving only the descriptions of the natural wonders, and this reference was cut out with the rest. Mr. Folsom also suggested the idea to General Washburn, of which fact Mr. N. P. Langford is still a living witness. From Mr. Folsom's suggestion, however, as from Mr. Catlin's, no direct result can be traced.

The next mention of the subject was in Mr. Langford's lecture, delivered, as already related, in Washington, January 19, 1871, in New York, January 21, 1871, and at a later date in Minneapolis. At each of these places he closed his lecture with a reference to the importance of setting apart this region as a national park. The *New York Tribune* of January 23, 1871, thus quotes Mr. Langford:

"This is probably the most remarkable region of natural attractions in the world; and, while we already have our Niagara and Yosemite, this new field of wonders should be at once withdrawn from occupancy, and set apart as a public National Park for the enjoyment of the American people for all time."

Such is the origin of the idea which has found realization in our present Yellowstone Park. The history of the Act of Dedication, by which the Park was created, may be briefly told. The general plan for a vigorous prosecution of the project was arranged in Helena, Montana, mainly by Nathaniel P. Langford, Cornelius Hedges, and William H. Clagett, who had just been elected delegate to Congress from Montana, and who had already himself independently urged the importance of converting this region into a public park. Mr. Langford went to Washington when Congress convened, and he and Mr. Clagett drew the Park Bill, except as to description of boundaries, which was furnished by Dr. Hayden. The bill was introduced in the House by Mr. Clagett, December 18, 1871. Senator Pomeroy, of Kansas, had expressed a desire to perform a like service in the Senate, and accordingly Mr. Clagett, as soon as he had presented the measure to the House, took a copy to the Senate chamber and gave it to Senator Pomeroy, who immediately introduced it. In each House it was referred to the Committee on Public Lands. In the Senate no formal report was prepared. In the House the Hon. Mark H. Dunnell, of Minnesota, chairman of the sub-committee having the bill in charge, addressed a letter under date of January 27, 1872, to the Secretary of the Interior, asking his opinion upon the proposed measure. The Secretary replied, under date of January 29, fully indorsing the project, and submitting a brief report by Dr. Hayden, which forcibly presented all the main features of the case.

The bill, being thus before Congress, was put through mainly by the efforts of three men, Dr. F. V. Hayden, N. P. Langford, and Delegate William H. Clagett. Dr. Hayden occupied a commanding position in this work, as representative of the government in the explorations of 1871. He was thoroughly familiar with the subject, and was equipped with an exhaustive collection of photographs and specimens gathered the previous summer. These were placed on exhibition and were probably seen by all members of Congress. They did a work which no other agency could do, and doubtless convinced every one who saw them that the region where such wonders existed should be carefully preserved to the people forever. Dr. Hayden gave to the cause the energy of a genuine enthusiasm, and his work that winter will always hold a prominent place in the history of the Park.

Mr. Langford, as already stated, had publicly advocated the measure in the previous winter. He had rendered service of the utmost importance, through his publications in *Scribner's Magazine* in the preceding May and June. Four hundred copies of these magazines were brought and placed upon the desks of members of Congress on the days when the measure was to be brought to vote. During the entire winter, Mr. Langford devoted much of his time to the promotion of this work.

The Hon. William H. Clagett, as delegate from the territory most directly interested in the passage of the bill, took an active personal part in its advocacy from beginning to end.

Through the efforts of these three gentlemen, and others less conspicuously identified with the work, this measure received perhaps the most thorough canvass of any bill that has ever passed Congress. All the members were personally visited and, with few exceptions, won to the cause. The result was a practical unanimity of opinion when the measure came to a vote. This first took place in the Senate, the bill being passed by that body January 30. It was warmly supported upon its passage by several members and opposed by one, Senator Cole, of California, a fact the more remarkable because that Senator had in his own state—in the preemption by private parties of the Yosemite wonderland—the most convincing example possible of the wisdom of such a measure as that proposed.

The Senate bill came up from the Speaker's table in the House of Representatives, February 27. Mr. Dunnell stated that the Committee on Public Lands had instructed him to ask the House to pass the Senate bill. Hon. H. L. Dawes, of Massachusetts, warmly advocated the measure, which was then passed by a decisive vote.* The bill received the President's signature March 1, 1872.

This subject has been treated somewhat in detail because there has long been a false impression among the people as to who it was that first put forward this important project. To no individual is the public more indebted for the creation of the Park than to Dr. F. V. Hayden, who was long prominently connected with the geological surveys of the government. But he did not, as is generally supposed, originate the idea. His statement in his report for 1878, Vol. II, p. xvii, that, "so far as is now known, the idea of setting apart a large tract about the sources of the Yellowstone River, as a National Park, originated with the writer," is entirely erroneous; and there is the less excuse for the error in that Dr. Hayden had himself heard the measure advocated by Mr. Langford in his Washington lecture. In fact, he is known to have said in later years, only a short time before his death, while residing in Philadelphia, that when the project was first talked of among the members of his party, in the summer of 1871, he personally disapproved it because he doubted the practicability of adequately guarding so vast a region; but that, upon further reflection, he became converted to the measure and was thereafter its most ardent advocate.

But it is not so much actual facts, as what men believe these facts to be, that controls human action; and it is unquestionably true that the above quotation correctly expresses the views of

* No yea and nay vote was taken in the Senate. The vote in the House was—yeas, 115; nays, 65; not voting, 65.

the great majority of members of Congress when the Park measure was before that body. It is not too much to say that Dr. Hayden's influence, as the official representative of the government, was a controlling factor in the passage of that measure.

Perhaps no act of our national Congress has received such general approbation at home or such profuse commendation from foreigners as that creating the Yellowstone National Park. The lapse of twenty years has only served to confirm and extend its importance and to give additional force to the sentiment so well expressed by the Earl of Dunraven when he visited the Park in 1874:

"All honor then to the United States for having bequeathed as a free gift to man the beauties and curiosities of 'Wonderland.' It was an act worthy of a great nation, and she will have her reward in the praise of the present army of tourists, no less than in the thanks of the generations of them yet to come."*

It was a notable act, not only on account of the transcendent importance of the territory it was designed to protect, but because it was a marked innovation in the traditional policy of governments. From time immemorial privileged classes have been protected by law in the withdrawal, for their exclusive enjoyment, of immense tracts for forests, parks, and game preserves. But never before was a region of such vast extent as the Yellowstone Park set apart for the use of all the people without distinction of rank or wealth.

The example thus set by the United States has been widely followed. We have now the Yosemite and Sequoia national parks, and numerous parks upon the sites of great battlefields. The State of New York has a Niagara Park and contemplates setting apart a portion of the Adirondac region. Minnesota has the Itasca State Park, including the sources of the Mississippi. Canada also has a public park at Niagara, and a large reservation in the midst of the finest scenery of the Rocky Mountains. New Zealand has set apart for public use the region of

* Earl of Dunraven, *The Great Divide* (London, Chatto and Windus, 1876), xi.

84

her hot springs and geysers. Finally the question is being mooted of reserving a vast tract of Africa wherein the large game of that continent may be kept from annihilation.

☆ 11 ☆

WHY SO LONG UNKNOWN?

THERE IS NO MORE singular fact connected with the history of the Upper Yellowstone country than its long immunity from the presence of white men. From the date when Lewis and Clark first stood at the Three Forks of the Missouri, less than one hundred miles distant from this notable region, sixty-five years elapsed before it was fully known. In the meantime all the surrounding country had been thoroughly explored. Cities, villages, farms, and highways had been established throughout the West. A railroad had been built across the continent. But around the head waters of the Yellowstone, the most attractive region of all, it was still *terra incognita*. A fact so remarkable requires adequate explanation.

The most difficult feature of the question is the fact that no knowledge of this region appears ever to have been derived from the Indians. Lewis and Clark were told of the Great Falls of the Missouri and of other notable geographical features long before they saw them. But of the far more wonderful falls of the Yellowstone, of the great lake in the mountains, or of the marvelous volcanic phenomena in the same neighborhood, they received no hint. There is not a single instance on record, so far as we can discover, except in the meager facts noted in an earlier chapter, where rumors of this strange country appear to have fallen from the lips of Indians. And yet it was not a region unknown to them, for they had certainly passed back and forth across it for a long period in the past. Their deep silence concerning it is therefore no less remarkable than mysterious.

But how was it that the long period of the fur trade should have passed without disclosing this country? To this question a more satisfactory answer may be returned. The Upper Yellowstone country was indeed, as we have seen, frequently visited in these early years. But it was never favorite territory. Old trappers say that, although it abounded in beaver, they were not so plentiful as in lower altitudes, while on the streams impregnated with mineral matter, the furs were not so good. The seasons also were unpropitious. The winter snows were so deep—they came so early and remained so late—that little could be done there except from the middle of June to the middle of September. But furs taken during the summer months are of inferior quality, and there was consequently no inducement to trap. Moreover it was generally at this time that the gatherings at posts and rendezvous took place, and after these were over but little time remained. Causes like these prevented extensive operations in this region, and doubtless only a comparatively small number of trappers ever saw it.

Then, the interest of the trader was against the dissemination of any knowledge which might induce immigration and hasten the certain ruin of his occupation. The stress of competition also caused him to remain silent concerning the places he had seen, lest a rival should profit thereby. He took no pains to reveal the country, and the trappers were too illiterate to do so had they wished. With the one notable exception which has been mentioned in a previous chapter, no important press notice of these regions appeared during the entire sixty-five years.[1]

The fur business itself quickly ran its course, and with it disappeared all probability of an early discovery of the geyser regions from this cause. The war with Mexico followed, with the vast cession of territory which it secured. Then came the highly important discovery of gold in California. Already the Mormon emigration had taken place. These great events completely changed the character and purpose of western explo-

1 In later editions, Chittenden changed this statement to the more accurate "With few notable exceptions . . . ."

87

ration. The whole West was forgotten, expecting only California and the Salt Lake Valley and the routes leading to them. None of these led close to the geyser regions. On the north were the British fur trader's route and the Missouri River route, both of which led directly west to the Columbia. To the south was the great thoroughfare along the Platte River and through South Pass, leading to Utah, California and Oregon. Still further south were the long known routes near the border of Old Mexico. It was hopelessly improbable that gold seekers bound to the Pacific Coast along any of these routes would stray into the mountain fastnesses about the sources of the Yellowstone.

Finally the whole energy of the government in the field of exploration was directed away from this region. In the period from 1804–1806, the date of Lewis and Clark's expedition, to 1870, the date of the real discovery of the Park, there were no fewer than one hundred and ten explorations in the country west of the Mississippi, nearly all of which had government authority and were conducted on a scientific basis. Of these, eighty-four were in the territory lately acquired from Mexico, and mostly in the far south and west. Nineteen were east of the Bighorn Mountains, five north of the Yellowstone, and only two in the region about the Upper Yellowstone. Of these two expeditions one was that of Lewis and Clark and was in no wise intended to explore the Upper Yellowstone further than might be necessary to find a good route to the Pacific. This leaves but a single expedition of the whole number, that of Captain Raynolds, which was directed to this specific territory. How the purpose of this expedition was defeated by the heavy snow in the mountains and by the solar eclipse of 1860 has been elsewhere related.

And so it came about that it was the gold-seeker who finally revealed the well-kept secret of the Yellowstone. Itself destitute of mineral wealth, this region could not escape the ubiquitous prospector. It was not, indeed, by him that it was publicly proclaimed to the world. He cared little for any country that was destitute of "color" or "pay." But the hints he dropped put others on the track and opened the door to real discovery.

This fact of long delay in the discovery of the Upper Yellowstone is the most important in its history. Had it been known at an earlier date, its fate would have been deplorably different. The period of the fur traders was too early for the interest of the people to demand, or the power of the government to enforce, its protection. If Captain Raynolds had discovered it, all its most valuable tracts would have been preempted long before the government would have been able to give it attention. Fortunately, the discovery was delayed until there was a considerable population in the country near by, and the government was prepared actively to consider the matter. Before settlers could establish a permanent foothold, the Park was created, and all the vexatious obstacles, which might otherwise have defeated the project, were avoided.

☆ 12 ☆

LATER EXPLORATIONS

As soon as the remarkable character of the country about the sources of the Yellowstone became generally known, there was a rush of explorers to its borders. Every expedition that could possibly extend the field of its labors in that direction did so, and there was scarcely a summer during the next twenty years that the Park was not the scene of some official exploration or visit.

By far the most important of these were the various expeditions under the United States Geological Survey. Dr. Hayden was again in the country with two parties in 1872 and very widely extended the range of observations of the previous year. In 1878, survey parties again entered the Park and resumed work there on a much more minute and extensive scale. The result of that year's explorations appeared in 1883 in the form of an elaborate report by Dr. Hayden and his coworkers which entered with much detail into the more important subject of scientific interest. It was embellished with a great number of engravings and colored plates and with an exhaustive series of topographical and geological maps. The work was again taken up in 1883 and was continued for several years. All questions of scientific importance were investigated more thoroughly than ever before, and many valuable official reports and monographs, together with a superb map, have been the result.

In 1872, General John Gibbon, U.S.A., with a considerable party, made a tour of the Park, passing by the usual route from Mammoth Hot Springs via Mt. Washburn, the Grand

Cañon, and the Lake, to the Firehole Geyser Basins. On his way home he attempted to ascend the north Fork of the Madison, following an old trail; but he abandoned the attempt after going a few miles. His name, which was given to the river, has also attached to many other features along that valley.

In 1873, Captain William A. Jones, of the Corps of Engineers, passed through the Park as part of a more extended reconnaissance. He was the first to carry a party through the "impassable barrier" of the Absaroka Range. Jones Creek, just east of the northern portion of the Yellowstone Lake, shows where the party entered the Park. From the Lake the expedition passed down the east bank of the river to the valley of Junction Butte; thence west to Mammoth Hot Springs; thence back over the usual trail via Tower Creek, Mt. Washburn, the Grand Cañon and Mud Geyser, to the Lower Geyser Basin; thence via the Upper Basin to the west shore of the Yellowstone Lake; thence to the Upper Yellowstone River; thence through Two-Ocean Pass and Two-Gwo-Tee Pass to the valley of Wind River. The chief results of this expedition, in the line of original discovery, were the passage of the Absaroka Range, the verification of the traditional "Two-Ocean Water," between Atlantic and Pacific Creeks, in Two-Ocean Pass, and the discovery of the extremely easy pass (Two-Gwo-Tee)* over the Continental Divide, between the Snake and Wind rivers. Prof. Theodore B. Comstock accompanied the expedition as geologist. A valuable report of the reconnaissance appeared in 1875.†

In 1875, Captain William Ludlow, of the Corps of Engineers, made a reconnaissance from Carroll, Montana, on the Missouri River, to the Yellowstone Park and return. In the Park he followed the previously traveled routes and developed little in the line of original discovery. He succeeded, however, in obtaining a very accurate measurement of the height of the Yellowstone Falls, and his report forms one of the ablest brief

* So named by Captain Jones for one of his Indian guides.

† Captain W. A. Jones, *Reconnaissance from Carroll, Montana, to the Yellowstone National Park* (Washington, Government Printing Office, 1876).

descriptions of the Park extant. Among his civil assistants was George Bird Grinnell, now widely known as the editor of *Forest and Stream,* and as one of the most steadfast and watchful guardians the Park has ever had.[1]

During the same season a distinguished party, consisting of the Secretary of War, Gen. W. W. Belknap, and several prominent officers and civilians, with Lieutenant G. C. Doane, of National Park fame, as guide, made a complete tour of the Park. An exceedingly interesting narrative of the trip was written by Gen. W. E. Strong, who was a member of the party.

In 1877, Gen. W. T. Sherman and staff made a tour of the Park. His letters on the subject to the Secretary of War, and the official report prepared by Gen. O. M. Poe of his staff, form a valuable contribution to the literature of the Park.

In the same year Gen. O. O. Howard crossed the reservation in pursuit of the Nez Percé Indians.

In 1880, the Hon. Carl Schurz, Secretary of the Interior, accompanied by Gen. Crook with a large number of officers and soldiers and an immense pack train, entered the Park from the valley of Henry Fork and made an extended tour.

In 1881, Captain W. S. Stanton, of the Corps of Engineers, made a reconnaissance through the Park, entering by the way of Soda Butte Creek and passing out by the Madison Valley. The most important result of his work in the Park was a more accurate table of distances over some of the routes than had previously been in use.

In July and August of this year, the Hon. John W. Hoyt, Governor of Wyoming, with a military escort under command of Major Julius W. Mason, U.S.A., made an extended reconnaissance to discover a practicable wagon route to the Yellowstone Park from the south-east. He entered the Park by way of the Upper Yellowstone, passed through it by way of Yellowstone and Shoshone lakes, the Firehole Geyser Basins, the Grand Cañon, the lower end of Yellowstone Lake, and left it along the route by which Captain Jones had entered in 1873.

[1] Grinnell, who was also an authority on the northern Plains Indians, especially the Cheyennes and Blackfeet, died in 1938.

In the years 1881 and 1882, General Sheridan, with parties of considerable size, twice crossed the Park and visited its most important points. His expeditions were of great value to the Park from the forcible warning which he gave to the public concerning the demoralized condition of its civil administration.

The most elaborate expedition that ever passed through this region took place in August, 1883.* It included among its members the President of the United States, the Secretary of War, the Lieutenant General of the Army, a United States senator, and several other distinguished officers and civilians. The interesting part of the journey lay between Fort Washakie, Wyo., and the Northern Pacific Railroad at Cinnabar, Mont. The party traveled entirely on horseback, accompanied by one of the most complete pack trains ever organized in this or any other country, and escorted by a full troop of cavalry. Couriers were stationed every twenty miles with fresh relays, and by this means communication was daily had with the outside world. The whole distance traveled was 350 miles, through some of the wildest, most rugged, and least settled portions of the West. No accident or drawback occurred to mar the pleasure of the expedition. The great pastime en route was trout fishing, in which the President and Senator Vest were acknowledged leaders. The phenomenal "catches" of these distinguished sportsmen might pass into history as typical "fish stories," were they not vouched for by the sober record of official dispatches, and the unerring evidence of photographer Haynes' camera. The elaborate equipment of this expedition, the eminent character of its personnel, and the evident respon-

* The year 1883 seems to have been the banner year for distinguished visitors to the Park. The list of arrivals for that year includes the President of the United States and a member of his cabinet; the Chief Justice and an associate justice of the United States Supreme Court; the General, Lieutenant General, and a large number of other distinguished officers of the army; six United States senators; one territorial governor; a prominent railroad president; the ministers from Great Britain and Germany; the President of the Admiralty Division of the High Court of Justice, England; three members of Parliament; and a considerable number of other eminent personages, both from this country and abroad.

93

sibility resting upon those who conducted it attracted a great deal of attention at the time and gave it a prominent place in the annals of Western Wyoming.

To these various expeditions must be added the extensive, though desultory, explorations of P. W. Norris during the five years that he was superintendent of the Park.

It has thus come about that the Yellowstone National Park, though remote, inaccessible, and of great extent, is about the most thoroughly explored section of the United States. Within the territory bounded by the 44th and 45th parallels of latitude, and the 110th and 111th meridians of longitude, there are nearly four hundred geographical names. The names of hot springs and geysers would probably double the number. To appreciate this fact, it must be remembered that there are no settlements in the Park, and that counties, townships, cities, and villages, which on ordinary maps form so large a portion of the names, are here entirely absent. That region has indeed been a paradise for the explorer, the topographer, and the geologist; and its splendid opportunities have not gone unimproved.

Although not strictly in the line of original exploration, the few winter journeys that have been made through the Park may nevertheless most appropriately be considered in this place, reserving for a later chapter a description of the difficult and hazardous nature of these undertakings. The first of these expeditions was in 1887, under the auspices of the *New York World,* and was led by Frederick Schwatka, the Arctic explorer. It was organized on a grand scale, "with Arctic 'sleeping bags,' the Norwegian 'ski,' the Canadian 'web' snow shoe, and toboggans to carry supplies, photographic equipment, and astronomical instruments." But the elaborate outfit proved fatal to the enterprise, which quickly resulted in a magnificent failure. The conditions were different from those in Arctic travel, and the recent fall of light snow negatived any attempt to move toboggans through it successfully. The party consumed three days in getting to Norris, a distance of twenty miles. Here Lieutenant Schwatka became ill and the expedition was abandoned.

But Mr. F. J. Haynes, the well known Park photographer, who had accompanied the party, resolved to continue the tour in order to secure a collection of winter views. Three other members of the party joined him. They abandoned the toboggan and strapped the baggage on their backs. They went by way of the usual route to the Upper Geyser Basin, where they were snow-bound for five days in a fearful blizzard. Thence they went to the Grand Cañon, and from that point over Mount Washburn to Yancey's.[2] On this part of the trip the party nearly lost their lives, wandering for three days in a blinding storm without food or shelter. The circuit covered about two hundred miles, and the temperature ranged from ten to fifty-two degrees below zero during the entire trip of twenty-nine days.

In March, 1894, two very important winter expeditions were made in the Park. Mr. F. J. Haynes went through for the purpose of extending his line of winter views, and also of photographing the Park game. Accompanying him was Felix Burgess, government scout.

Following this party by a few days, and joining it at the Grand Cañon, came another party with a staff correspondent of *Forest and Stream*. This gentleman, Mr. E. Hough, of Chicago, Ill., made the entire round of the Park, studying its game and other similar matters.[*] His narrative, published in *Forest and Stream*, forms one of the most entertaining and valuable contributions yet made to the literature of the Park. These two expeditions played an important part in securing the enactment of the National Park Protective Act, in May, 1894.

2 Yancey's was a hostelery and was also the name for the general area bounded by Crescent Hill, Mount Washburn, Speciman Ridge, and the mountains north of the Lamar River.

* Emerson Hough, "Forest and Stream's Yellowstone Park Game Exploration," *Forest and Stream,* Vol. XLIII (Thirteen articles, spring and summer issues, 1894).

13

AN INDIAN CAMPAIGN
THROUGH THE YELLOWSTONE PARK

IN A LETTER dated at Fort Ellis, Montana Territory, August 19, 1877, addressed to the Hon. George W. McCreary, Secretary of War, the writer, General W. T. Sherman, then on a tour of inspection of the "country north of the Union Pacific Railroad," tells of his recent visit to the Yellowstone National Park. This was about the period when our Indian wars in the Far West were at their height. Only a year had elapsed since the Custer massacre. It was the crisis of the Indian military question. There was at that time scarcely a spot in the whole Missouri and Yellowstone valleys that was safe from Indian depredations. Naturally, therefore, General Sherman had his mind upon this subject when his small party, comparatively unprotected, were traveling through the wilds of the National Park. But he saw nothing there to excite his fears, and in the letter above referred to, says: "We saw no signs of Indians and felt at no moment more sense of danger than we do here." It will presently be seen how delusive was this fancied security, and by how narrow a margin it escaped resulting disastrously to the General's party.

The tour from Fort Ellis to the Park and return had taken from August 4 to August 18. On the latter date, the party met an ingoing company of tourists from Helena composed of the following persons: A. J. Weikert, Richard Dietrich, Frederic Pfister, Joseph Roberts, Charles Kenck, Jack Stewart, August Foller, Leslie Wilke, L. Duncan, and Benjamin Stone (colored cook). The party followed the usual route to the Grand Cañon and Falls of the Yellowstone, where they were in camp August 24.

As they were entering the territory of the Park, another party was on the point of leaving it after a tour of about two weeks. This party was composed of the following persons, most of whom were from Radersburg, Montana: George F. Cowan and wife, Frank and Ida Carpenter, brother and sister of Mrs. Cowan, Charles Mann, William Dingee, Albert Oldham, A. J. Arnold, and a Mr. Meyers. They had formed a permanent camp in the Lower Geyser Basin, where the Fountain Hotel now stands,[1] and from that point had made daily short excursions to the various localities of interest. They all visited the geyser basins and some of the party crossed to the Lake and Cañon of the Yellowstone. They must have been seen by Sherman's party, for they were directly in his route. The party had completed their tour of the Park, August 23, and had arranged to set out for home early on the following morning.

In order to understand the unfortunate turn which the affairs of these two tourist parties were about to take, it will be necessary to explain, in briefest outline, the cause and previous incidents of one of the most remarkable Indian campaigns in our history.

From the time of Lewis and Clark, the Nez Percé Indians had dwelt in what are now the states of Oregon, Washington, and Idaho. Their territory extended from the Salmon River on the south to the Pelouse River on the north, and from the Bitter Root Mountains westward into the present states of Idaho and Washington. In 1855, they ceded to the United States a part of their territory, and the principal chiefs located in the several portions of the remainder. In 1860, gold was discovered on the reservation and the usual gold rush followed. The danger of a conflict with the Indians became so great that a temporary arrangement, pending action by the government, was made between them and their Indian agent, opening a portion of the reservation "to the whites in common with the Indians for mining purposes."

But the settlers did not stop with these concessions. In defiance of law, they built the town of Lewiston on the reser-

[1] The Fountain Hotel has since been dismantled.

97

vation and gave other proofs of their project for permanent occupancy. It soon became necessary for the government to take some decisive step, and this was accomplished in 1863 by a new treaty in which the Indians relinquished three of their most important valleys, the Wallowa, the Alpowai, and the Salmon River.

The treaty, however, was far from receiving the general assent of all the chiefs. A formidable faction, headed by Chiefs Joseph, Looking Glass, Big Thunder, White Bird, and others, refused to be bound by it, and were henceforth referred to in official reports as the "Non-treaty Nez Percés." For a time the authorities made no effort to enforce the new treaty, and the Indians were "tacitly permitted to roam" over their ancient hunting-grounds.

This condition of affairs continued for thirteen years with various efforts in the meantime to arrive at some more satisfactory settlement. Finally, in 1876, a civil and military commission was appointed to visit the Nez Percé Indians, to examine into their grievances, and to determine what measures were necessary for a permanent settlement of the question. The report* of this Commission is interesting, both for the facts it relates in regard to the tribal life and characteristics of the Nez Percé Indians, and for the heroic treatment of the long-standing troubles which it recommends.

These Indians were altogether a peculiar people. The early missionaries had converted them to the Christian faith, and, whether from that cause, or from natural proclivity, they were among the most religious of our Indian tribes. There is a general concensus of authorities that, despite certain grave defects of character, they were, mentally and morally, far above the average Indian. In later times, approaching the period covered by this sketch, they fell under the influence of a class of mystics called "dreamers" who taught a doctrine of land own-

* "Report of Civil and Military Commission to Inquire into Grievances of the Nez Perce Indians," *Annual Report of the Secretary of the Interior for 1877* (Washington, Government Printing Office, 1877), Part 1, 607.

ership which was the immediate cause of all their subsequent troubles. This doctrine was, in substance, that "the 'Creative Power,' when he made the earth, made no marks, no lines of division or separation, upon it, and that it should be allowed to remain as it is"; that it "should not be disturbed by man, and that any cultivation of the soil, or other improvements, any voluntary submission to the control of government," were incompatible with the true purpose for which it was made. At bottom it was the broad principle that no man or aggregation of men can take from other men the right to enjoy what nature has made free for all. Why the Commission should characterize this doctrine as "pernicious," unless a thing is pernicious whenever it is impracticable, is not easy to understand. From the point of view of the nomadic life of the redmen, it is hard to conceive a theory of land tenure, or the want of it, more nearly approaching a perfect ideal.

Unfortunately for such a doctrine, at the point at which American history had now arrived, it was no longer possible of realization; and any attempt to put it in force could not result otherwise than in failure. So it was with Joseph and his followers. The government for a long time overlooked their infractions of the Treaty of 1863 but finally was compelled to interfere. The Commission recommended that the existing treaty be enforced, by military aid if necessary. The recommendation was approved, and to General O. O. Howard fell the task of putting the Indians on their proper reservation.

For a time it seemed that they would be induced to submit without the employment of active force; but just as success was apparently assured, the Indians murdered some twenty white men, women, and children in revenge for one of their number killed the previous year. Peaceful negotiations came at once to an end, and the military authorities assumed control of the situation. This was June 13, 1877.

Between that date and July 12th, three battles were fought in which both sides suffered severely, and the Indians displayed extraordinary fighting ability. They then left their country—

as it proved, not to return—and set out across the mountains to their oft-visited "buffalo country," in the Judith Basin, far to the eastward of the Upper Missouri.

But their route lay too close to the military post of Fort Missoula and to the towns in the more thickly settled portions of Montana. They bore off to the southward, through a country with whose people they were well acquainted, and with whom they had often traded in previous excursions to the buffalo country. Here they found friends and obtained the supplies they needed.

In the meantime, General Gibbon with a small force, which he had gathered from Forts Benton, Shaw, and Missoula, and from volunteers among Montana citizens, was in close pursuit. He overtook the Indians on the Big Hole River, in South-western Montana, where a desperate battle ensued in which his own force was severely handled.

The Indians then passed south into Idaho with Howard in pursuit, swung around to the east, and recrossed into Montana by way of Henry Lake. Near Camas Creek, they had an engagement with the pursuing troops.

Howard arrived at Henry Lake at 8:00 A.M., August 23, just as the Indians had left. The long marches compelled him to halt at this point for three or four days, to rest his men, and replenish his supplies. This gave the Indians a considerable start, of which, however, they took only a leisurely advantage. Their route lay across the Yellowstone Park, which they entered by Targhee Pass, and on the night of August 23 they encamped on the Firehole River, in the Yellowstone National Park, a short distance from where we left the Radersburg tourists and less than twenty miles from the camp of the Helena party. The interest of the campaign for the next week centers chiefly upon the fortunes of these unlucky excursionists.

Before sunrise on the morning of August 24, Arnold and Dingee, who had got up to prepare the camp fire, saw Indians approaching. The rest of the party were promptly aroused. The Indians at first professed to be friendly, and little alarm was felt;

but the party nevertheless had no appetite for breakfast, and immediately broke camp and started down the river toward home. But they were soon surrounded by the increasing number of Indians, who began to give indications that trouble was at hand. They were told that it would be unsafe to proceed down stream further, that the only course was to turn back with the Indians. This they were soon forced to do. After traveling some two miles up Nez Percé Creek, it became impossible to take the wagons further. The horses were unhitched and the ladies mounted upon them, and in this manner the march was resumed. At this point Mr. Frank Carpenter was induced to hasten to the front in search of Chief Looking Glass to see if he could not secure the party's release; but his suspicions becoming soon aroused, he refused to go further, and returned. In fact, it turned out later that Looking Glass was not in front at the time and that the pretense that he was was a mere subterfuge to aid in scattering the party. The captives were now taken up the East Fork of the Firehole (Nez Percé Creek) to the foot of Mary Mountain, where a consultation with the chiefs was had. Mr. Cowan was spokesman for the whites, and Poker Joe, who knew English well, for the Indians. The party were here set at liberty, their horses, guns, and ammunition were taken, they were given other horses instead, and, just as the Indians were about to resume their march, they were told to depart by the back trail. After proceeding some three-fourths of a mile, they were overtaken by some seventy-five young and war-painted bucks, and were compelled to countermarch. It was about this time that two of the party were given a hint by a friendly Indian and made their escape in the brush. The rest continued their way back to the point where they had been liberated and some distance beyond in the direction of Mary Lake. Just as they reached the first sharp ascent of the mountain about 2:00 P.M., in the midst of dense timber, the attack began. At the first fire Cowan was struck in the thigh and fell from his horse. His wife instantly rushed to his side, threw her arms around his neck, and strenuously resisted the

Indians in their further attempts to kill him. But they partially pulled her away and an Indian shot Cowan again in the head. He was then left for dead.

In the meantime, Carpenter had had a narrow escape. A young Indian had drawn his revolver upon him, when Carpenter, remembering his religion, quickly made a sign of the cross. He was then hid by the Indians in a clump of underbrush until the trouble was over, and was assured that the ladies should not be harmed.*

The other members of the party scattered promptly when the firing began. All of them escaped to the brush, but one of them was wounded in the attempt and fell behind a log where he lay concealed until the Indians had gone.

This left Carpenter and his two sisters captive. They were taken along with the Indians, each being lashed to a pony behind an Indian. The captives became separated and did not see each other until ten o'clock that night at the Indian camp near Mary Lake. The next day, August 25, the march was resumed, and the party were taken across the Yellowstone at the ford near Mud Geyser. Here Carpenter's fate was put to a vote of the chiefs and by a majority of one he was given his life. In the afternoon, the ladies were given each a pony, and, with Carpenter, were escorted by Poker Joe back across the river. They were then taken a mile down stream and told to depart— instructions which they obeyed with no want of alacrity.

Strange to say, none of the party had been killed. Cowan, who had been twice shot, and stoned also by the Indians, when they saw lingering evidences of life, nevertheless survived. About five o'clock in the afternoon he recovered consciousness and drew himself up by the bow of a tree, when lo!, close behind him was another Indian with his rifle ready to fire. He

---

* The Indians denied that Carpenter was saved because of making a sign of the cross, although they remembered his making it. The chiefs had strictly enjoined their followers that the whites were not to be injured. When the few lawless bucks began the attack, some of the other Indians interfered. Poker Joe was sent back by the chiefs for the same purpose when they surmised what was going on. He succeeded in preventing further trouble, and Carpenter's escape was due to this cause.

tried to get away, but the Indian fired and the ball passed through his left hip. He now gave up hope as he fell again to the ground. The Indian, however, did not come up. After waiting until every one had apparently gone, Cowan crawled along till about midnight, seeking a place of greater safety, and then waited for day. At daybreak he commenced crawling back toward the old camp, a distance of eight or ten miles. He passed the abandoned wagons on the way, where he found a dog belonging to the party. It took him four days to reach the old camp, but once there he found matches, coffee, and some other articles which helped him to keep alive. The day after his arrival, he was picked up by Howard's scouts.

Arnold, who had escaped to the brush before Cowan was shot and had wandered for four days until finally picked up by Howard's command near Henry Lake, came along with the troops on the twenty-ninth, and remained with Cowan until their arrival in Bozeman. They were taken by Howard to near Baronett's Bridge,[2] and then sent down the river.

Already Carpenter and his sisters had made their way down the river, passing close to the camp of the other party of tourists near the Falls—whom they might have saved had they chanced to see them—and were met by a party of soldiers under Lieutenant Schofield twelve miles from Mammoth Hot Springs. They were escorted to the springs, whence they went to Bottler's ranch, some distance below the Park, and a short time afterward returned to Radersburg. It was about two weeks before Mrs. Cowan learned that her husband was still alive. After all these miraculous escapes, it is interesting to know that Mr. Cowan and his wife survived to make another tour of the Park a few years later under better conditions.

It will not be necessary to follow in detail the fortunes of the rest of the party. They all escaped, though with much suffering, in their wanderings through the wilderness.

When the captive members of the party were being marched down the Yellowstone slope east of Mary Lake, they heard considerable firing in the timber to their right. This is thought

2 At the junction of the Lamar (or East Fork) with the Yellowstone.

to have been an attack upon two prospectors who were known to have been in the neighborhood at the time, and who have never since been heard of.

The party of Helena tourists in camp near the Falls of the Yellowstone on the night of August 24, were less fortunate than the Radersburg party. On the morning of the twenty-fifth, they started up the river toward the Mud Geyser. They had gone about a mile beyond Sulphur Mountain when they discovered moving bodies of men, part of whom were fording the river. Careful scrutiny showed them to be Indians, and the party rightly divined that they must be the hostile Nez Percés. They hastily retraced their steps and went into camp in the timber near the forks of Otter Creek, about a mile and a half above the Upper Falls of the Yellowstone. Here they remained undisturbed all day and the following night. On the morning of the twenty-sixth, Weikert and Wilkie set out to scout the country. They went as far as Sulphur Mountain and, finding everything clear, started back to camp to report. When entering the timber just north of Alum Creek, they suddenly met a band of Indians who promptly opened fire on them. A flight and pursuit of considerable duration ended in the escape of both men, but not until Weikert had been wounded. This party of Indians had just attacked and dispersed the group in camp. They had stolen upon the camp as dinner was being prepared, and a volley of musketry was the first warning the tourists had of their presence. There was instant flight and most of the party managed to get away. But Kenck was soon overtaken and killed; and Stewart after being severely wounded, prevailed on the Indians to spare his life.

Weikert and Wilkie, who had hastened back to camp after their own encounter, found everything in confusion and all the party gone. They soon fell in with several of them, and together they set out for Mammoth Hot Springs.

And now began another series of wanderings through the trackless wilderness of the Park. Two of the party made their way by way of the Madison River, where they were given food by soldiers, to Virginia City, and thence to Helena. The rest of the survivors after much hardship reached Mammoth Hot Springs, and soon after left the Park with the exception of Weikert, Dietrich, the colored cook, Stone, and a man named Stoner.

On August 31, Weikert and one McCartney, owner of the first hotel ever built in the Park, went to the Falls of the Yellowstone in order if possible to learn the fate of the missing members of the party. Shortly after their departure from the Springs a band of Indians prowled across the country from the Yellowstone to the Gardiner and went down the latter stream as far as Henderson's ranch near the present town of Cinnabar. After a brief skirmish and a general pillage here, they went back to Mammoth Hot Springs. Stoner and the colored cook fled precipitately, but Dietrich, believing the Indians to be friendly scouts, remained behind and was shot dead in the door of the hotel. Stone made a lucky escape by climbing a tree, and his subsequent ludicrous recital of his experience became a standing jest among the inhabitants of the Yellowstone.

Weikert and McCartney went back to the old camp on Otter Creek, where they buried Kenck's remains and gathered up whatever of value the Indians had left. On their way back, when on the head waters of Black Tail Deer Creek, they met the band of Indians who had just slain Dietrich at Mammoth Hot Springs. A lively skirmish ensued in which Weikert lost his horse. The two men succeeded in finding refuge in some neighboring brushwood.

Just as the Indians went into camp on the night of August 23, their first day in the Park, they captured one Shively, who was on his way to Montana from the Black Hills. As Shively professed to know the country, which the Nez Percés had never seen before, they impressed him into their service as guide. He was with them thirteen days and claims to have served them faithfully, as well as to have received fair treatment from them. At any rate he won their confidence by his behavior, and was watched so carelessly that he escaped one dark night just as the Indians were crossing the north-east boundary of the Park.

As soon as the command at Henry Lake had become recuperated, the pursuit was vigorously resumed. Howard followed in the track of the Indians as far as to the ford of the Yellowstone; but instead of crossing at this point, he descended the river by the left bank to the site of Baronett's celebrated first bridge over the Yellowstone. From the Lower Geyser Basin to this bridge a road had to be opened for the wagons. It was a prodigious undertaking, but was performed with astonishing rapidity under the direction of Capt. W. F. Spurgin, twenty-first Infantry. The bridge was found partially destroyed by the Indians and had to be repaired, after which the line of march was continued up the Lamar and Soda Butte valleys, and across the divide to the valley of Clark's Fork.

The authorities had been widely warned of the probable route of the Indians and were lying in wait to intercept them. Gen. Sturgis expected to do this as they emerged from the Absaroka Mountains; but unfortunately he stationed himself in the wrong pass and left the one which the Indians took unguarded. By this loss of time he fell in behind both the Indians and Howard, who was now in close pursuit. The Indians crossed the Yellowstone September 12. Here Sturgis overtook them with a company of cavalry, and a slight conflict ensued. The Indians then struck north, apparently for the British line. On September 23 they crossed the Missouri at Cow Island and resumed their march north. But they were intercepted by Gen. Miles in the Bear Paw Mountains, and a severe fight followed, at the northern base of the range on Snake Creek, less than thirty miles from the boundary.[3] The Indians were utterly defeated and Looking Glass was killed. Most of the survivors surrendered unconditionally and the rest escaped across the line. This was on October 5, 1877.

Since the first outbreak, June 13, three months and twenty-two days had elapsed. The flight and pursuit had extended over 1,500 miles. There had been no fewer than fifteen engagements. The whites had lost 6 officers and 121 soldiers and citizens killed, and 13 officers and 127 soldiers and citizens

[3] It was closer to forty miles from the boundary. Merrill D. Beal, *"I Will Fight No More Forever": Chief Joseph and the Nez Perce War*, 205.

LOOKING GLASS, NEZ PERCÉ CHIEF
KILLED AT BEAR PAW MOUNTAIN

" . . . the Nez Percés staked their all on a single throw. They lost, and were irretrievably ruined."

W. H. Jackson Photograph
Smithsonian Institution

MAMMOTH HOT SPRINGS

". . . a place where hell bubbled up."

Yellowstone National Park Photo

LOWER FALLS OF THE YELLOWSTONE

"The remainder of this day, August 30, and the next were spent
in exploring the cañon and measuring the heights of the falls."

Yellowstone National Park Photo

OLD FAITHFUL GEYSER

" 'Old Faithful,' as if forewarned of the approach of her distinguished visitors, gave them her most graceful salutation; and thus she bowed out the era of tradition and fable and ushered the civilized world into the untrodden empire of the Fire King."

GEORGE CATLIN, OIL SELF-PORTRAIT DONE IN 1825

". . . the project of creating a vast national park in the West originated with George Catlin . . . ."

Thomas Gilcrease Institute
of American History and Art

GENERAL HENRY DANA WASHBURN

"It was during his residence in Montana that the famous Yellowstone Expedition of 1870 took place. His part in that important work is perhaps the most notable feature of his career. As leader of the expedition he won the admiration and affection of its members."

From N. P. Langford, *The Discovery of Yellowstone Park*

FERDINAND VANDIVEER HAYDEN, SEATED

"To no individual is the public more indebted for the creation of the Park than to Dr. F. V. Hayden, who was long prominently connected with the geological surveys of the government."

W. H. Jackson Photograph
Yellowstone Library and Museum Association

NATHANIEL PITT LANGFORD
FIRST SUPERINTENDENT OF YELLOWSTONE NATIONAL PARK

"He has always been its [the Park's] ardent friend, and his enthusiasm upon the subject in the earlier days of its history drew upon him the mild raillery of his friends, who were wont to call him 'National Park' Langford—a soubriquet to which the initials of his real name readily lent themselves."

From D. E. Folsom, "The Folsom-Cook Exploration of the Upper Yellowstone in the Year 1869," Vol. V in *Contributions to the Historical Society of Montana* wounded. A large part of the Indian losses could never be ascertained, but their known losses were 151 killed, 88 wounded, and 489 captured.

This celebrated campaign is well intended to elicit the fullest sympathy for the unfortunate Nez Percés. A vast deal of sentiment has been wasted upon the cause of the red man. Opinions have ranged from the extreme views of Catlin, who could see no wrong in the Indian, to those of the rabid frontiersman whose creed was "no good Indian but a dead one." But, if there ever was a case where sympathy might well incline to the side of the Indian, it is the one under consideration.

The Nez Percés had always been friendly to the whites, and it was their boast that they had never slain a white man. They were intelligent, brave, and humane. In this campaign they bought supplies which they might have confiscated; they saved property which they might have destroyed; they spared hundreds of lives which other Indians would have sacrificed. If some of the more lawless element committed various outrages, they might justly reply that the whites had fired into their tents where their women and children were sleeping. In short, their conduct in this campaign places them in all respects vastly nearer the standard of civilized people than any other of the native tribes of the continent.

In estimating the causes that led to the war, history can not fail to establish that the Indians were in the right. It was a last desperate stand against the inevitable destiny which was robbing the Indian of his empire, a final protest against the intolerable encroachments of the pale face. In defense of this principle, the Nez Percés staked their all on a single throw. They lost, and were irretrievably ruined. They were transported to a distant territory, and the land of their fathers they saw no more.*

The campaign of 1877 was the only one in which tourists of

---

* After the surrender, Joseph and a few of his followers were sent to Fort Leavenworth, where they remained until July, 1878, when they were taken to the Indian Territory. After languishing here for seven years, they were established on the Colville Reservation in Washington.

the National Park were ever subjected to serious danger from the Indians. It has left its mark indelibly upon the Park. "Nez Percé Creek" will always remind the traveler of the terrible danger in which another party of tourists was once placed upon the borders of that stream. "Howard's Trail" will not soon be effaced from the forests and mountains where Captain Spurgin, with brilliant expedition, built the first passable highway through that tangled wilderness.

In 1878, there was a slight alarm in the Park caused by an ephemeral raid of the Bannock Indians; but, beyond the loss of a few horses, no damage was done.

14

ADMINISTRATIVE HISTORY OF THE PARK

THE ACT OF DEDICATION of the Yellowstone National Park indicates in clear terms the purposes for which it was created. These are:

(1) The preservation of its natural curiosities, its forests, and its game.

(2) The reservation of its territory from private occupancy so that it may remain in unrestricted freedom "for the benefit and enjoyment of the people."

(3) The granting of such leases and other privileges as may be necessary for the comfort and convenience of visitors.

One grave omission in the original act, and the long-continued failure of Congress to remedy it by subsequent legislation, in a large degree nullified these important purposes. Strange as it may seem, for twenty-two years, or until the spring of 1894, there was no law defining offenses in the Park or providing a penalty for their commission. Wanton vandalism, destruction of game, or burning of forests could be visited with no heavier punishment than ejection from the Park and confiscation of "outfit." In the reports of every superintendent, for more than a score of years, this condition of affairs was brought to the attention of Congress. Meanwhile there were experienced all the evils of a license which at times was wholly unchecked and which has never until very recently been under proper control.

This long-standing misfortune was aggravated by another scarcely less serious—the failure of Congress for several years to appropriate funds for the protection and improvement of the Park. For this failure, however, no one can justly be held faultily responsible. The promoters of the Park project had based extravagant expectations upon the results to be derived from leases. They believed that the revenue from this source would amply cover the expense of opening the necessary highways and providing a proper police force. They did not make due allowance for the fact that there was at that time no railroad within 500 miles, that the new reservation was an almost impassable wilderness, and that the construction of roads and bridges must necessarily precede any profitable tourist business. Neither do they seem to have realized that these leases could not, in the nature of things, yield a revenue commensurate with the work of opening up so wild and extensive a country. The argument of self-support was a mistaken one. It did an important work, however, for it is doubtful if Congress would have created this reservation had it not believed that no additional public burden was to be incurred thereby.

The subsequent results of this erroneous impression were in every way unfortunate. It was several years (1872 to 1878) before any money was appropriated for the Park, which, in the meanwhile, was left wholly without means for its improvement and protection. The Secretary of the Interior might indeed publish rules and regulations for its government, but they could avail but little so long as there was no authority to carry them into execution. In fact, the only valuable result of the creation of the Park during these years was the exclusion of settlers from its territory.

Shortly after the Park was created, the Hon. N. P. Langford was appointed its first superintendent. The selection was in every sense an admirable one. Mr. Langford had been a member of the famous Washburn Expedition and an earnest worker in securing the Act of Dedication. He was intimately acquainted with all phases of western life, and was an enthusiast upon the subject of his new charge. But, from the first, his hands were completely tied. No money was ever allowed him for his services nor for any other form of expenditure in the interests of the Park. He was, therefore, powerless to accomplish effective work. His office, which he held for about five years, was a source of great annoyance to him; for he was frequently, and most unjustly, charged in the public press with the responsibility for a condition of things for which he was in no sense to blame.

In 1877, there appeared, as Mr. Langford's successor, one of the most unique and picturesque, as well as one of the most important, characters in the history of the Park. This was Philetus W. Norris, of Michigan. He was appointed immediately upon the advent of President Hayes's administration, and held office very nearly five years, or almost exactly the same length of time as his predecessor.

Norris filled with varying capacity the roles of explorer, path-finder, poet, and historian in the Park. He was a man of extraordinary energy, and, if not in the fullest sense a practical man, he had at least the invaluable quality of being able to produce results. He entered upon his new field of duty with a genuine enthusiasm, and he was fortunate in receiving from Congress substantial means with which to carry out his plans.

The work of Norris' administration may be conveniently considered under three heads: his discoveries, his road building, and his reports.

He was pre-eminently an explorer. He not only traveled repeatedly over all the known trails, but he penetrated the unknown sections of the Park in every direction. Though not the discoverer, he first made generally known the geyser basin that bears his name. He explored and reported upon the Hoodoo region, and first called prominent attention to the noble cañon of the Middle Gardiner. But the most important feature of his explorations was the study he made of the history and antiquities of the Park. We owe more to him than to any one else for evidence of the former presence of white men in that region. His discoveries also in the matter of prehistoric races and of early Indian history possess scientific value.

In the role of road builder, Norris was a pioneer in the Park. Before his time, wagons could get up the Gardiner to Mammoth Hot Springs, and up the Madison to the Lower Geyser Basin. He opened the way direct from Mammoth Hot Springs to the Upper Geyser Basin, from the Lower Basin to the Yellowstone River, Lake, and Falls, and from Mammoth Hot Springs to Tower Creek. He thus shortened the old pack-train route by one-third, and foreshadowed the general road system which Lieutenant Kingman later formulated into a permanent project of improvement. As a road engineer, he was not a distinguished success. His work was ill-conceived and poorly executed, but at the same time it gave access to many places wholly inaccessible before. All the difference between poor roads and none at all may justly be placed to his credit.

The third and most important feature of Norris' work was his official reports and other writings. As he was always doing something, although seldom in the best way, so he was always saying something, with the same constitutional defect. Nevertheless, he has left in his five annual reports a great deal of useful information, which he supplemented by a long series of articles in the *Norris Suburban,* a paper at that time largely read throughout the West. It is not too much to say that he was a prime mover in the strong awakening of public sentiment in regard to the Park, which began to show itself toward the close of his administration.

Norris' work in the Yellowstone Park can not be passed over without praise. It left its mark, as its author did his name, in every quarter. But one thing must be charged to his account— an almost total failure to *protect* the Park. He did, indeed, by his public utterances, denounce the vandalism and game destruction that were then rampant; but he did little in a practical way to prevent them—no more, in fact, than his predecessor, although he was given the means.

Norris was succeeded in February, 1882, by Patrick H. Conger, of Iowa. Of this Superintendent, it need only be said that his administration was throughout characterized by a weakness and inefficiency which brought the Park to the lowest ebb of its fortunes, and drew forth the severe condemnation of visitors and public officials alike. This administration is an important one, however, for it marks the period of change in public sentiment already referred to, and the commencement of reform in the government of the reservation.

As if the unfortunate condition of affairs due to the lack of suitable laws for the reservation were not enough, there arose in the early part of Superintendent Conger's administration a new and even more formidable danger, under the euphemistic title of the Yellowstone Park Improvement Company. Previous to this time, there had been no regular leases in the Park. Several informal permits for occupancy had been granted, and a small number of inferior buildings had been erected. In 1880, there were nine of these buildings, nearly all of them being plain log cabins, with earth roofs, of the common frontier pattern. Only two, the headquarters building at Mammoth Hot Springs and Marshall's Hotel in the Lower Geyser Basin, rose in dignity above the primitive type. No one as yet thought of remaining in the Park during the winter season.

But it finally dawned upon certain sagacious individuals that here was a rare opportunity to exploit the government for their private emolument under the generous guise of improving the Park and catering to the comfort of the tourist. A company was accordingly formed, and a valuable ally secured in the person of the Assistant Secretary of the Interior, who granted a lease of 4,400 acres in tracts of about a square mile at each of the great points of interest. It was urged in defense of this sweeping grant, that it was hoped in that way to secure the protection which had yet failed to be found by any other method. It was thought that if responsible parties could be given exclusive control of these natural curiosities, they would, at least from motives of self-interest, preserve them. But such a monopolistic privilege was clearly opposed to the spirit of the Act of Dedication. Why set apart this region for the free and unrestricted enjoyment of the people, if the Secretary of the Interior could give to private parties absolute control of all its most important localities? Was this a proper interpretation of "small parcels of ground," as specified in the Act? The danger involved in this action was indeed a grave one, and it at once aroused a storm of protest throughout the country.

It was about this time also that there began to appear those various railroad and segregation projects which from that time to the present have been a formidable menace to the continued existence of the Park. A more extensive consideration of this particular subject is reserved for a later chapter.

It thus became apparent as early as 1882 that immediate and radical measures must be adopted if the Park was to be preserved in its original condition. General Sheridan, who passed through that region in 1881, 1882, and 1883, gave forcible warning of the impending danger and urgently appealed to the public sentiment of the country in favor of some action which should avert it. The Governor of Montana made an earnest appeal to Congress. Other influential voices united in the same cause, and already it was broadly hinted that the only salvation of the Park lay in turning it over to the military. The whole matter was brought prominently before the next Congress, and in March, 1883, a clause in the Sundry Civil Bill containing the annual appropriation for the Park forbade the granting of leases of more than ten acres to any single party, authorized the Secretary of the Interior to call upon the Secretary of War for troops to patrol the Park, and provided for the employment of ten assistant superintendents who were to constitute a police force. Thus was the bold scheme of the Improvement Company frustrated, and the foundation laid for the present administrative system. The Secretary of the Interior, however, seems not to have wished to avail himself of military assistance, and it was several years before this provision of the law was put into operation.

It was in this same year that the killing of birds and animals in the Park and the taking of fish by any other method than by hook and line were absolutely prohibited. Previously, hunting had been allowed so far as was necessary to supply the wants of camping parties—a concession that practically operated as an unrestricted license.

The failure of Congress to enact needed legislation at length became so nearly chronic that relief was sought in another

114

direction. Nearly all the territory of the Park, and all its great attractions, were within the limits of Wyoming. Might it not therefore be within the province of territorial legislation to furnish the necessary legal protection? The subject was agitated, and in the winter of 1884, an act was passed, designed "to protect and preserve the timber, game, fish, and natural curiosities of the Park," and for other purposes. The act was very stringent in its provisions, and clearly indicated the deep-seated nature of the disease which it was designed to cure. But it totally failed of its purpose. The attempt at territorial control of what was really a national institution was in itself a grave blunder. Then, the officials chosen to execute the law seem to have been poorly qualified for the purpose, and to have displayed lamentable want of tact and moderation. Some of their arrests were so tyrannical and inexcusable as to create universal protest. The spectacle of the assistant superintendents—federal officials—sharing, as informers, the fines levied by a territorial court, was not designed to create respect for the new authority. At length the unpopularity of the law became so extreme, that it was repealed March 10, 1886.

Although so unwise a measure could not stand, the first effect of its repeal was to advertise the fact that the Park was practically without legal protection. Matters became even worse than before. The common verdict, as gathered from official reports and other sources, is that the body of police, styled assistant superintendents, were notoriously inefficient if not positively corrupt. They were, for the most part, creatures of political favoritism, and were totally unused to the service required of them. Commissioned as guardians of the rarest natural wonders on the globe, they not infrequently made merchandise of the treasures which they were appointed to preserve. Under their surveillance, vandalism was practically unchecked, and the slaughter of game was carried on for private profit almost in sight of the superintendent's quarters. Already some of the rarer species of animals had suffered a depletion in numbers from which they have never recovered; and the prediction of Prof. Comstock, in 1874, seemed on the

115

point of realization, that "the zoological record of to-day" was about to "pass into the domain of the paleontologist."

The difficulties that beset the administration of the Park seem to have been too great for Superintendent Conger to grapple with successfully, and he resigned, July 28, 1884. It may at least be said in his favor, that, weak as his management had been, no charge of corruption or dishonesty was ever brought against him.

In his place was appointed, August 4, 1884, Robert E. Carpenter, of Iowa. Mr. Carpenter's views of the requirements of his office were clear and positive, and he promptly set about to carry them into execution. In his opinion, the Park was created to be an instrument of profit to those who were shrewd enough to grasp the opportunity. Its protection and improvement were matters of secondary consideration. Instead of remaining at his post during the winter season, he went to Washington, and there, in concert with a member of the Improvement Company, very nearly succeeded in carrying a measure through Congress by which important tracts upon the Reservation were to be thrown open to private occupancy. So confident of success were these conspirators that they even located claims upon the tracts in question, and their names appeared on claim notices posted to designate the localities. Fortunately the measure failed of passage, but the scandal of Superintendent Carpenter's conduct led to his prompt removal from office.

On the day of his removal, May 29, 1885, Colonel David W. Wear, of Missouri, was appointed to the vacancy. Colonel Wear appears to have been admirably fitted for the place. He at once set out to reform the administration of the Park, and his intelligent and vigorous measures gave the highest encouragement to those who had been familiar with the previous condition of affairs. But, as has often happened before, and will often happen again, he was made to suffer for the sins of his predecessors. The bad repute into which the government of the Park had fallen was not easily removed, and Congress finally declined to appropriate money for a protection which

116

did not protect. The Secretary of the Interior was thus compelled to call upon the Secretary of War for assistance. The regime of civilian superintendents passed away, and that of the military superintendents began. The change was bitterly opposed by the Secretary of the Interior and by all who held or hoped to hold places under the old order; but the sequel quickly proved the wisdom of this action of Congress. The old order necessarily felt the evil of our patronage system of officeholding; but no single act ever went so far to eliminate this fruitful source of misfortune as the assignment of the administrative control of the Park to the officers and soldiers of the army.

August 20, 1886, marks the turning point in the administrative history of the Reservation. It was upon that day that Captain Moses Harris, First U.S. Cavalry, relieved the civilian superintendent of his duties, and soldiers supplanted the so-called assistant superintendents as a Park police. Henceforth an entirely new order was to obtain. It was to be seen how much could be accomplished, even in the absence of laws, toward a vigorous and healthful administration. Trespassers upon the Reservation were promptly removed. The regulations were revised and extended, printed upon cloth, and posted in all parts of the Park; and their violation was visited with summary punishment to the full extent of the superintendent's authority. Abuses of leasehold rights were searchingly inquired into and reported to the department. As soon as this show of real authority was made manifest, and it became apparent that here was a man who meant what he said, a great part of the difficulty was over. Nothing in fact conduces so much to the infraction of law as a belief in the incompetency or dishonesty of those delegated to enforce it, and the removal of this cause was a long step in the right direction.

The Park was particularly fortunate in its first military Superintendent. Captain Harris possessed in a marked degree the qualities required for that position. He was vigorous and uncompromising in suppressing lawlessness, just and impartial in his rulings, and untiring in his watchfulness for the public

117

interest. Although his immediate superior, the Secretary of the Interior, had strenuously opposed the installation of the military in the Park, he never failed to pay a high tribute to the efficiency with which the new Superintendent performed his duties. In fact, this high opinion of Captain Harris' services was soon shared by all who were familiar with the situation. Even *Forest and Stream,* whose fidelity to the best interests of the Park has been a distinguishing feature of that journal for the past fifteen years, was fain to admit, although it had regarded the change as impolitic, that under Captain Harris' guardianship "the Park had been cared for as it never had been before."

Captain Harris remained in charge for nearly three years, and was succeeded, June 1, 1889, by Captain F. A. Boutelle, First U.S. Cavalry. That the evil of political interference and private intriguing was not yet wholly eliminated from the affairs of the Park became manifest when Captain Boutelle undertook to enforce the regulations against a prominent employee of the hotel company. For causes not publicly understood, he was unexpectedly relieved from duty January 21, 1891, and Captain George S. Anderson, Sixth U.S. Cavalry, the present Superintendent, was assigned in his place.

Going back now to the Yellowstone Park Improvement Company, the history of that erratic concern will be briefly traced. It is important first to state, however, that the conduct of private business in the Park has, until recent years, been most unsatisfactory. The Park was long unfortunate in the men who sought to carry on business within its borders, and even yet it is not wholly free from the evil of unscrupulous and dishonest schemers. The strife, backbiting, struggle to ruin each other, which seemed to be the chief purpose of those who at first sought government favors on the Reservation, can be understood only by those who have seen them, or have gone to the trouble to examine official correspondence. More than once has the government made these troubles the subject of special investigation, although generally with indifferent results.

The new hotel company had a meteoric career, promising great things, but effecting no permanent improvement except the partial construction of the Mammoth Hot Springs Hotel. Its fortunes early collapsed, and the opening of the tourist season of 1885 found the great building in the possession of unpaid workmen, who held it under a kind of military guard until their wages should be paid.

This company, and other lesser concerns, gradually transferred their rights to a new company, called the Yellowstone Park Association, which is still in operation. It is largely identified with the Northern Pacific Railroad, and although it has a practical monopoly of the tourist business, it has never subjected itself to the charge of using that monopoly to the disadvantage of the public. From the old and unsatisfactory condition of things it has built up a hotel system which, though incomplete, is far ahead of what could be reasonably expected in a region so remote from the great centers of civilization.

It was in the early part of Conger's administration that the government took up in earnest the question of road construction. For some years, the public, thoroughly weary of Norris' roads, had been urging the necessity of sending an engineer officer to take charge of that important matter. This agitation bore fruit in 1883 in the assignment of Lieutenant D. C. Kingman, of the Corps of Engineers, to the charge of this work. His tour of duty ran through three years and resulted in the greatest improvement to the road system. He prepared the project which has served as a basis of all subsequent work, and he did much toward carrying it into execution. His reports were especially valuable, not only in matters connected with his particular work, but also those pertaining to the general welfare of the Reservation. He was among the first to lift a warning voice against the grave danger of railroad encroachment, and no one since his time has presented this matter in a more convincing light.

The years 1894 and 1895 have brought a radical improvement to the administrative status of the Park. May 4, 1894, the long desired code of laws was enacted. On August 3 of the same year, an act was passed further regulating the question of leases and removing the most serious defects of previous legislation. In the autumn of the same year, the road work was taken from the charge of a non-resident engineer with headquarters in St. Paul, and placed in direct charge of the Superintendent, thus bringing the entire administrative control under a single head.

These two years have also witnessed a decided check to the schemes of those who still persist in believing that the Park was created for their personal aggrandizement. Strong adverse reports have been submitted, practically for the first time, by Congressional committees against the so-called Segregation project, the admission of railroads into the Park, and the construction of an electric railway therein.

With the exception of the lack of a sufficient force of scouts properly to patrol that region, the condition of affairs on the Reservation is now eminently satisfactory—far more so than at any previous period.

15

THE NATIONAL PARK PROTECTIVE ACT

ONE OF THE MOST IMPORTANT milestones in the history of the Park has been so recently set that the public is as yet not fully conscious of its existence. It has already been stated that for more than twenty years the Park was wholly without adequate statutory protection; and that this long-standing defect was finally remedied by the enactment of a comprehensive measure in the spring of 1894. The circumstances attending the passage of this act, and the prompt manner in which a great misfortune was changed into a lasting benefit, form one of those singular instances of good fortune which have so largely characterized the history of this region.

Bills providing suitable protection for the Park were introduced at the first session of the Fifty-third Congress, just as they have been for the past twenty years, and apparently with not much greater chance of success. The wanton recklessness of those who seek special privileges in the Park, and are unwilling that any measure for its welfare shall pass unless coupled with their own private schemes, threatened this time, as hitherto, to defeat congressional action. But an unforeseen event, of such powerful bearing as practically to override all opposition, occurred in March, 1894, and quickly brought about the desired consummation.

It is well known that the only herd of bison, now roaming in their native condition within the present limits of the United States, is in the Yellowstone National Park.[1] There has always

1 Today there are about 6,000 bison in the United States, and over 800 in the magnificent Yellowstone Park herd.

been a lively interest in the preservation of this herd, and its extinction would be regarded as a deplorable calamity. With proper protection, it will undoubtedly flourish, but there is no margin for carelessness or neglect.

During the winter of 1894, Captain George S. Anderson, U.S.A., superintendent of the Park, learned that snow-shoe tracks had been seen along Astringent Creek in the Pelican Valley east of the Yellowstone River, in territory ranged over by the buffalo in winter. The same tracks were seen near Soda Butte station pointing toward Cooke City. Inquiry proved them to have been made by one Howell, a well known poacher and lawless character, who was evidently driving his trade in the winter buffalo country. It was apparent that he had left the Park for supplies and would soon return. Captain Anderson accordingly laid his plans for capture.

There has been given a brief account of the winter expedition through the Park in the spring of 1894, of which Mr. F. J. Haynes and Scout Burgess were members. Burgess was instructed to examine the country east of the Yellowstone and obtain, if possible, a clue to Howell's whereabouts. Early on the morning of March 12, he set out from the Lake hotel with a single companion. Private Troike, of the Sixth Cavalry, and before it was scarcely daylight struck a dim snow-shoe trail in the valley of Astringent Creek. Soon after, he found the poacher's tepee and a number of buffalo heads hung up, by means of a pulley, to the limb of a tree so as to be out of the reach of wolves. Every thing indicated that the poacher was there for a business of some duration and magnitude.

Leaving the teepe [sic] and following Howell's morning trail for some distance, Burgess' attention was soon arrested by six rifle reports. These six shots slew five buffalo. Burgess soon discovered Howell engaged in skinning the head of one of the buffalo. His rifle was leaning against another some fifteen feet from him. A dog (but this Burgess did not know) was coiled up under the leg of a buffalo. Burgess thus had the dangerous duty to perform of crossing the intervening space of some four hundred yards, where there was no cover and where he might easily be seen by Howell or the dog. Considering the desperate character of these poachers, and the fact that Burgess was armed only with a revolver as against Howell's rifle, the peril involved in this capture may be easily appreciated. But fortune was on Burgess' side. A heavy storm was on, and the wind was blowing direct from Howell to Burgess. This prevented the dog from scenting approach and Howell from hearing any noise from the leeward. Burgess did not stop to reckon the chances of success, but promptly sallied forth upon his intended victim. On his way he ran upon an open ditch about ten feet wide. To make a snow-shoe jump on level ground is a feat of much difficulty, but Burgess managed to accomplish it. By good fortune nothing happened to arouse Howell, and Burgess got within fifteen feet of him before he was aware that there was anyone within as many miles. With Burgess' cocked revolver over him, he discreetly surrendered. Private Troike was summoned, the rifle and accouterments were seized, and the party set out at once for the Lake hotel. But such are the difficulties of snow-shoe travel in this region, that it was long after dark before they reached their destination.

The Yellowstone Park Association keeps a solitary watchman at each of its hotels during winter and has a telephone line connecting each with Mammoth Hot Springs. By virtue of this lucky fact, Howell's capture, though made some sixty miles from the nearest telegraph station, and in a region where winter travel is impossible except on snow shoes, was made known to the Superintendent before 9:30 P.M. that day. By another stroke of good fortune a representative of *Forest and Stream* was at that moment present at Mammoth Hot Springs. He had arrived but two days before and remained a guest of the Superintendent prior to a tour of the Park, which began two days later. The news of Howell's capture was at once put on the wire, and in less than twenty-four hours, *Forest and Stream* was represented in Washington with a new and powerful argument for the passage of the Offenses Bill. The imminent danger of the speedy and entire extinction of the only remaining herd of buffalo in the country produced the desired effect in Congress, and on May 7, 1894, the bill became a law.

It was throughout a most fortunate combination of circumstances that made this consummation possible. A Superintendent thoroughly devoted to the care of his important charge, and fearless in the execution of his duty; a scout who had the nerve to make an arrest full of peril to himself; the existence of a winter telephone line to the heart of that inaccessible region; the presence at Mammoth Hot Springs of a representative of that journal which holds first rank among the protectors of the Park; and uncommon good luck in minor details, caused this important event to cast its influence into the national councils almost before the echo of the poacher's rifle shots had died away among the mountains. Howell's act was a misfortune—a grievous misfortune—to the game interests of the Park; but its immediate result in legislation will prove a benefit of far greater consequence.

Howell was brought to Mammoth Hot Springs and was there imprisoned in the Fort Yellowstone guardhouse, and his case reported to Washington. As there was no law for his trial and punishment, the Secretary of the Interior in due time ordered his release. He was accordingly put out of the Park and forbidden to return without permission. But with his habitual disregard of authority, he came back the following summer and was discovered by the Superintendent in a barber's chair at Mammoth Hot Springs Hotel. He was promptly arrested and tried under the new law for violating the orders of the Superintendent in returning. He was convicted and sentenced to one month's imprisonment and fifty dollars fine. He thus became the Park Haman—first to be hanged upon the gallows of his own building.

Howell appealed the case to the U.S. District Court sitting at Cheyenne, Wyoming, and was released upon the technical ground that, as the prohibition against returning to the Park was merely an order from the Superintendent and not explicitly authorized by the regulations of the Secretary of the Interior, the offense did not come within the purview of the law. This defect in the regulations has since been remedied and the conviction of Howell, therefore, notwithstanding his final release, has all the force of precedent.

☆ 16 [1] ☆

HOSTILITY TO THE PARK

FROM WHAT HAS BEEN thus far set forth the reader can not have failed to observe how fortunate have been the events, both in prehistoric and in recent times, which have made the Yellowstone National Park what it is to-day. In the course of long ages Nature developed this region into its present attractive form, and filled it with wonders which will never fail to command the admiration of men. She placed it upon the very apex of the continent and made of it an inexhaustible reservoir of water for a perennial supply to the parched and rainless desert around it. She interspersed among its forests an abundance of parks and valleys where the native fauna of the continent, elsewhere fast passing away, may find protection in all future time. With infinite foresight she made it unfit for the gainful occupations of men, so that every motive to appropriate it for private use is removed.

For many years after the white man first looked within its borders, a rare combination of circumstances prevailed to keep it from becoming generally known until the time had arrived when the government could effectually reserve it from settlement. Finally, since its formal erection into a public park, the same good fortune has attended it, in spite of many adverse influences, until it has become thoroughly intrenched in the good opinion of the people.

So fully has the experience of the past quarter century confirmed the wisdom of setting apart this region for public uses,

1 Part II, "Descriptive," has been omitted (for it is hopelessly out of date), and in the original edition this was Chapter I of Part III.

126

that it ought no longer to be necessary to say a word in favor of its continued preservation. To most people it will seem impossible that there should be any one who would seek the mutilation or destruction of this important reservation. Unfotunately there are many such. No session of Congress for twenty years has been free from attempted legislation hostile to the Park. The schemes to convert it into an instrument of private greed have been many, and strange as it may seem, they are invariably put forward by those very communities to whom the Park is, and must ever remain, the chief glory of their section. It is a lamentable proof of the dearth of patriotic spirit that always betrays itself whenever the interests of individuals and of the public come into collision. Nevertheless it is a great satisfaction to know that this spirit of hostility is confined to an infinitesimal portion of the whole people. Excepting a few mine owners and their following, a handful of poachers, one or two railroad corporations, and a few greedy applicants for special franchises, the people of the country are a unit in favor of the strictest preservation of this great national pleasure ground. No better proof of this can be had than the fact that the Park has successfully withstood for so long a period every attack that has been made upon it.

It will not do, however, to assume that because these schemes have hitherto failed, they will always continue to fail. Since they have their origin in speculative ventures, they will be put forward so long as they offer the least pecuniary inducement. The certainty of this, and the danger of their ultimate success, justify the assignment of a brief space to a consideration of this subject.

☆ 17 ☆

RAILROAD ENCROACHMENT AND CHANGE
OF BOUNDARY

NEARLY ALL OF THE ENTERPRISES that have been put forward in opposition to the true interests of the Reservation partake of the nature of railroad encroachment. Without entering into the merits of particular projects, it will be sufficient to explain in general terms the reasons why the government has always opposed them.

Railroads in the Yellowstone Park are objectionable because:

(1) They will mar, and in places destroy, that natural condition which is one of its greatest charms. From the first it has been the wish of those who know any thing of the Yellowstone that it should remain as nature made it. The instructions of the Interior Department to the first Superintendent of the Park, two months after the Act of Dedication became a law, thus announced the policy of the government upon this subject:

"It is not the desire of the Department that any attempts shall be made to beautify or adorn this reservation, but merely to preserve from injury or spoliation the timber, mineral deposits, and various curiosities of that region, so far as possible, in their natural condition."

It requires no argument to show that nothing would so interfere with this natural condition as the construction of a railroad through that country, and the danger involved in these projects early became apparent to all who were well acquainted with the situation. As early as 1883, Lieutenant Kingman thus refers to this subject in his annual report, wherein he describes his proposed road system for the Park:

128

"The plan for improvement which I have submitted is given in the earnest hope and upon the supposition that it [the Park] will be preserved as nearly as may be as the hand of nature left it—a source of pleasure to all who visit it, and a source of wealth to no one. If the Park ever becomes truly popular and national, it will be when the people come to know and appreciate its delightful summer climate, the wonderful efficiency of its baths and its mineral waters, as well as the natural wonders, beauties and curiosities to be seen there. Then, if there are numerous small, quiet hotels scattered here and there throughout the Park, where visitors can have plain and simple accommodations at moderate prices, the overworked and the sick, as well as the curious, will come here, not to be awed by the great falls and astounded by the geysers, and then to go away, but will come here and will remain for weeks and months, and will find what they seek, rest, recreation and health. But if it ever becomes the resort of fashion, if its forests are stripped to rear mammoth hotels, if the race-course, the drinking saloon and gambling-table invade it, if its valleys are scarred by railroads, and its hills pierced by tunnels, if its purity and quiet are destroyed and broken by the noise and smoke of the locomotive; . . . then it will cease to belong to the whole people, and will interest only those that it helps to enrich, and will be unworthy the care and protection of the National Government."

The history of the twelve years since the above was written confirms in every point this forcible presentation of the case.

(2) Railroads will unavoidably seriously cripple the present tourist routes. They must of necessity occupy the valleys. But it is through these that the tourist route passes, and it is frequently the case that they are not wide enough for both. In many cases the roadway would be forced back upon the hills, and in others its present location would have to be changed. It is certain that the admirable system of roads, which the government is slowly working out, would receive irreparable injury at the hands of any railroad which might be built through that region.

129

(3) Railroads would mean the inevitable destruction of the large game. The winter snows are too deep among the hills for game to subsist there. It is necessary to come down into the valleys, where there is more grass and less snow. But, as already stated, it is through these valleys that railroads must pass if at all. The trains would frighten the animals back into the hills, where starvation would await them. Moreover the loss of game from poaching would be greatly aggravated by the increased facility of clandestine access to that region.

(4) Railroads would destroy the Park forests. During July, August, and September, there are always long periods of dry weather when the dense bodies of fallen timber, the impenetrable tangles of underbrush, and the luxuriant prairie grass are a mass of inflammable tinder. A spark converts it into a conflagration. A railroad winding its way through this country would render protection against fires, even now a matter of great difficulty, wholly out of the question. Referring to this subject in his annual report for 1894, the Superintendent of the Park says:

"Six months from the entrance of the first locomotive within the limits of the Park, there will not be one acre of its magnificent forests left unburned."

What such a catastrophe would mean to the future development of the surrounding country may be appreciated by a perusal of our chapter on the Flora of the Yellowstone.[1]

(5) As a matter of public policy, the granting of a railway franchise in the Park is objectionable because it necessarily creates a perpetual monopoly of a public privilege. There is no practicable way to avoid it. It has been proposed to compel the railroad to share the advantage of this monopoly with the public, by paying a certain percentage of earnings on its Park business to constitute an improvement fund. With Union Pacific history fresh in the public mind, the government will not be likely to enter into a partnership of that precarious nature.

From the foregoing exposition, it is clear that only the most cogent reasons should ever sanction the construction of rail-

[1] This chapter has been omitted in the present edition.

roads in the Yellowstone Park. These reasons, from the standpoint of the railroad companies, as set forth by the promoters of a recent bill before Congress, fall under two heads.

In the first place, it is speciously urged that a railroad would render the Park more accessible, cheapen the cost of visiting it, and make it fulfill more perfectly its original design as a park for the people. To all this it may be replied that the people do not want the improvement at the price they must pay for it. By an almost unanimous voice they oppose it. It is true that the Park is not as accessible as one might wish it to be, or as it soon will be. But to make it easily accessible, it is by no means necessary that a railroad should pass through it. A line touching the southern boundary and communicating with the central portions of the country would answer every practical purpose. The pretext that a railroad across the Reservation will greatly aid the tourist is erroneous. The points of interest are so scattered about that a coach would be in any case a necessity, and all the railroad would really save to the tourist would be the distance from the boundary to the belt line.[2]

Neither will such a railroad materially lessen the cost of a visit, which has always been, and will always be, in the main, getting *to* that region. The Reservation is 1,500 miles from the center of population of the country, and it is this remote location that makes visiting it cost. The outlay after getting there is trifling in comparison with that of coming and going. Whether a railroad pass through the Park, or simply touch its southern border, will not appreciably affect this principal item.

In the second place, it is urged that the Park stands directly in the path of the railroads and so "acts as a blockade to the development of three large states." As this will always form the staple argument for granting a right-of-way for railroads across the Reservation, it will be well to scrutinize it somewhat carefully.

It is not at all a question of whether the country about the Park is at present sufficiently supplied with railroads. The im-

2 The "belt line" is reference to the road system being constructed at that time within the Park.

portant question is: Will any portion of this territory be better served by a railroad that may be built across the Reservation than by one coming from another direction? The most superficial examination of the map, even by one not personally acquainted with the country, will answer this question in the negative. The Yellowstone Valley on the north, the Bighorn Valley on the east, the Jackson Lake country on the south, and the Madison and Henry Fork valleys on the west, find their natural outlets by routes not passing through the Yellowstone Park. A railroad entering the Park on one side through a lofty wall of mountains, and leaving it on the other through a similar wall, after traversing the inclosed plateau for a distance of perhaps seventy-five or one hundred miles, would be almost as much lost to the country outside as if for this whole distance it were built through a tunnel. In fact, the true welfare both of the Park and of the surrounding country would be best served by a line passing through the Wind River Valley, across one of the easy passes into the Valley of the Snake, and thence along the southern border of the Park, past Jackson Lake and the northern spur of the Teton Range, into the valleys of Idaho and Montana. This would give the Park a needed southern approach, and would directly serve a vast tract of territory. Tributary either to this line, or to one north of the Park, or to both, another would soon be built along the extensive Valley of the Bighorn. No imaginable route across the National Park could so well subserve both local and public interests.

From an engineering point of view, the Yellowstone Park is poor railroad country. It could be crossed, to be sure, but not easily, and not at all except by monopolizing portions of the tourist route. The long winter season of nearly seven months would interpose an almost insuperable obstacle to the successful operation of any line which might be built. We quote again from the report of the Park Superintendent for the year 1894:

"The great amount of moisture furnished by the lake and its numerous tributaries gives a mantle of snow that will average fifteen feet in depth, and with the strong winds prevailing in this mountainous country no railroad could be kept running during the six months of winter without being entirely inclosed in snow sheds, which would prove destructive to the natural beauty of the Park."

In short, it is certain that, were it not for the special inducements which a monopoly of Park travel offers, no railroad could afford to locate its line across that territory.

Closely related to this general subject is that of building an electric line for tourist transportation within the Park. It is at once apparent that the objections to such a railroad are much less formidable than to one operated by steam locomotives. The danger of fire is eliminated. The unsightly character of an ordinary railway outfit is exchanged for attractive tourist cars. The power plant, being located in cañons and operated by water, would give no outward evidence of its existence. There being no long trains of cars, no smoke, no screeching of locomotives, the game would not be much more frightened by it than by the stage coaches. In winter, traffic would be suspended and the game would be undisturbed on the ranges. The line, by its greater speed, would be a convenience to tourists having but a short time at their disposal, and also to those, infirm in health, who find the long stage rides fatiguing.

Such are the merits of an electric railway for tourist transportation in this country. If the people really desired it, and if it could be built and operated by the government, so as to exclude as far as possible all corporate management of Park business, there would be no serious objection to the project. Of course it should never be permitted, as some times proposed, to use the present wagon roads. These must not in any event be interfered with.

The question then is, do the people desire this kind of transportation? Fortunately we can answer this question with authority. In 1892, a vote upon it was obtained from the tourists of that season. The result was a majority of more than five to one against it. In giving their votes, tourists frequently went beyond the specific question at issue to express their emphatic disapproval of the construction of any kind of railroad in the

Park. The whole result was a gratifying proof of the deep-seated interest of the people in this Reservation, and of their unalterable wish that it remain forever free from the handiwork of man. In fact, to almost everybody in these days, a coaching tour like that through the Yellowstone, is a decided novelty. There is no other place in this country, probably not in the world, where one approaching it can be had. The people enjoy it. They would prefer to see it developed and perfected, rather than replaced by the noisy car, to get away from which they have come so far.

In the long and fruitless struggle to secure rights-of-way for railroads, the promoters of these projects have resorted to various indirect methods the most noteworthy of which is a proposal to change the boundary line of the Park. We have elsewhere explained how this boundary was originally determined. For a random line, which of necessity it largely was, it was a most excellent one. No one would have been dissatisfied with it were it not that it was subsequently found to stand in the way of certain private enterprises.

When it became apparent that the government would never consent to the construction of a railroad within the Park, it was sought to compass the same end by cutting off all that portion of the Reservation lying outside of, and including, the proposed right-of-way.

In accordance with the proverbial policy of indirection which characterizes schemes of this sort, the real purpose of this proposition is always veiled under a beneficent guise, intended to make its promoters appear as zealous guardians of the Park, rather than what they really are—conspirators for its destruction. The proposed change of boundary is ostensibly based upon the alleged necessity of having a natural boundary —that is, a boundary along the courses of streams. The present line, it is urged, is unmarked and no one knows where it is. A stream is a definite, visible line, seen and known by every one.*

* It is of course unnecessary to point out that an artificial line can easily be marked so that there shall be no uncertainty about its location. The

The pernicious fallacy that lurks in this argument is plainly visible if we look a little beneath the surface. *Never permit the boundaries of the Yellowstone Park to be brought down into the valleys.* Nature has indeed built the proper boundaries; but they are mountain ranges, not valleys. A thousand Chinese walls heaped together would not form a barrier like the Absarokas on the east, the Snowy Range on the north, the Galatin Range on the west, and the Tetons and the Big Game Ridge on the south. Along the present boundary line there are very few places where it is possible to build human habitations. No poacher or law breaker can there fix his stealthy abode ready at a favorable opportunity to dash across it. But if it were in the bottom of the valleys, a whole colony of these dangerous individuals would soon infest every border of the Park. Police surveillance, in any case extremely difficult, would then be well-nigh impossible. No! Whatever changes may be made in the boundary of the Park, let it always be kept among the mountain tops.

What the success of any of these projects to cut off, or segregate, portions of the Park would mean, may be judged from a single instance—that, namely, of the north-east corner of the Park. In this strip of territory are some of the finest scenery and most interesting scientific curiosities to be found upon the Reservation. It is the great winter grazing ground for the elk, and by estimate based upon actual count no fewer than 20,000 of these noble animals find their winter subsistence here. That all of this game would be almost instantly annihilated by the segregation of this strip goes without saying. More than this, the admission to the very heart of the Park of that class of reckless characters, who even now are its greatest source of danger, would vastly enhance the difficulty of protecting the remaining portions.

hollowness of purpose on the part of those who propose this argument is disclosed by the fact that, of the 280 miles, more or less, in the proposed boundary, they provide a natural line for only about 50 miles—or along that precise portion where they want to build a railroad. All the rest of the way an artificial line is good enough!

It is well to emphasize by repetition the few important facts pertaining to this question:

(1) There are no private interests on the borders of the Park whose development is jeopardized by the refusal of the government to give access to them by a railroad across the Reservation. They can all be reached from the outside without encountering greater obstacles than have been overcome in scores of other places throughout the West.

(2) There is no need of a railroad in the Park so far as the comfort or advantage of the tourists is concerned. A line along the southern border would answer quite as well, and would serve the surrounding country better.

(3) There is no occasion to construct an electric line in the Park. Nearly all of those who visit that region oppose it.

(4) There is no necessity for changing the present boundaries of the Reservation.

☆ **18** ☆

CONCLUSION

IT IS IN RESPECT OF the foregoing matters that the Yellowstone National Park has most to fear. The general public, although always in favor of its preservation, knows nothing of the merit of these various projects. A bill is introduced in Congress in the interest of some private enterprise. It is supported by representations and statistics gotten up for the occasion. There may be no one at hand to refute them, and they are the only information upon which Congress can act. More than once these bills have been reported favorably from committee, when every essential statement in the committee's report was contrary to fact. Unless some friend of the Park is present, ready and willing to devote time, and perhaps money, to its defense, there is only too much danger that these measures will eventually prove successful.

Thus far the Park has never been lacking in such friends; and there is no more encouraging fact in its history than this, that some one has always been on guard against any thing which might work to its injury. Men like Senator Vest in official position, or William Hallett Phillips in private life, and journals like *Forest and Stream* have stood for years, in a purely public-spirited manner, without remunerative inducement of any sort, and often in face of the bitterest vituperation and abuse, against the designs of selfish and unscrupulous schemers. In like manner, government officials connected with the Park have always, with one or two exceptions, earnestly opposed these dangerous projects. It is plain to any one who is familiar with its inside history, that, but for the agencies

137

just mentioned, there would not be to-day any Yellowstone Park at all. It is equally plain, that so long as friends like these are forthcoming, the Park has little to fear from its enemies.

In still another respect, the Park has been unfortunate where it had a right to expect better things. Prior to the admission of Montana, Wyoming, and Idaho into the Union of States, its interests were looked after in Congress, particularly in the Senate, by a few members who took great pride in promoting its welfare. But when the above territories were admitted to the Union, these gentlemen very naturally turned over the charge, which they had voluntarily assumed, to the members from the new States, as being thereafter its proper guardians. It was, of course, believed that in them, if in any one, the Park would find needed championship and protection. It is a matter of great regret that these very reasonable expectations have not been realized. A glance at the list of bills pertaining to the Yellowstone National Park, which have been presented to Congress in the past six years, will show that nearly every objectionable measure has been fathered by the very men whose first duty would seem to have been to oppose them. In a speech opposing the Segregation Project, delivered in the Senate in the winter of 1892–93, Senator Vest referred to this subject with justifiable indignation. He said:

"When those states [Montana, Wyoming, and Idaho] were territories, and not represented in the Senate, I considered it the duty of every senator, as this Park belonged to all the people of the United States, . . . to defend its integrity, and to keep it for the purposes for which it was originally designed. Since senators have come from those states, who, of course, must be supposed to know more about that Park than those of us who live at a distance, and since they have manifested a disposition to mutilate it, I must confess that my interest in it has rather flagged, and I feel very much disposed, in plain language, to wash my hands of the whole business. If the constituencies, who are more benefited than any others can possibly be in the Park, are willing to see it cut off, the best disposition of the matter would be to turn it open to the public, let the full greed and avarice of the country have their scope, let the geysers be divided out and taken for the purpose of washing clothes, . . . let the water of that splendid waterfall in the Yellowstone River be used to turn machinery, let the timber be cut off; in other words, destroy the Park, and make it a sacrifice to the greed of this advanced age in which we live."

It is only fair to say that generally these members do not personally favor the measures to which they lend official countenance and comfort. One can find a practical, if not a morally justifiable, excuse for their course in the exigencies of political life which too often constrain men to official action not in accordance with their private judgment. Unquestionably, a majority of the people of these young and enterprising states are immovably opposed to any thing which may tend to mutilate or destroy this important reservation; and it is not believed that their broader patriotism will ever be overridden by the narrow and perverted wishes of a few straggling constituencies.*

Finally, the effect of a single evil precedent upon the future of the Park must be kept constantly in mind. The door once opened, though by ever so small a degree, can not again be closed; but will sooner or later be thrown wide open. A privilege granted to one can not be denied to another. If one corner of the Park is cut off, other portions will share the same fate. If one railroad is granted a right of way across the reservation, another can not be refused. The only way to avoid these dangers is to keep the door entirely closed.

There is now but little real need of further positive legislation. Some provision should of course be made for an adequate

* The almost prophetic warning of Captain Harris in his last report as superintendent of the Park has a peculiar force in this connection:

"In my experience in connection with this National Park, I have been very forcibly impressed with the danger to which it is subjected by the greed of private enterprise. All local influence centers in schemes whereby the Park can be used for pecuniary advantage. In the unsurpassed grandeur of its natural condition, it is the pride and glory of the nation; but if, under the guise of improvement, selfish interests are permitted to make merchandise of its wonders and beauties, it will inevitably become a by-word and a reproach."

police force, and ample means should be provided to perfect the system of roads. Happily this duty involves no appreciable burden. It requires no continuing outlay to "beautify and adorn." And when it is done, the further policy of the government toward the Park should be strictly negative, designed solely to preserve it unimpaired, as its founders intended, for the "benefit and enjoyment" of succeeding generations.

GEOGRAPHICAL NAMES IN THE
YELLOWSTONE NATIONAL PARK

I

Introductory

IN COMMON EXPERIENCE, the importance of geographical names lies in their use as a means of identification. To describe an object there must be a name, and for this purpose one name is as good as another. But if the reason be sought why a particular name happened to be selected, it will generally be found to arise, not from this practical necessity, but from some primary fact or tradition, or from some distinguished character in the annals of the community where it occurs. In its mountains and valleys, its lakes and streams, and in its civil divisions, the cradle history of a country may always be found recorded.

In newly-discovered countries, the naming of geographical features is the dearest prerogative of the explorer, as it is also the one most liable to abuse from personal vanity or egotism. The desire to attach his name, or those of his personal friends, to the prominent land-marks of the globe, where the eye of posterity may never escape them, is a weakness from which no discoverer has yet shown himself free.

In a region like the Yellowstone National Park, destined for all time to be a resort for the lovers of science and pleasure, this temptation was quite irresistible, so much so that when the expeditions of 1870 and 1871 left the field, they left little worth naming behind them. And yet the honor thus gained has not, we venture to say, been all that its votaries desired. Small is the number of tourists who stop to inquire for whom Mary Lake, DeLacy Creek, or Stevenson Island was named. Fewer still are aware that Mt. Everts was *not* christened in honor of a distinguished American statesman of similar name, but in commemoration of one of the most thrilling individual experiences in American history. So with all these personal names. The lively satisfaction with which they were given finds no counterpart in the languid indifference with which the modern visitor mechanically repeats them.

In as much as it fell to the lot of the United States Geological Survey to originate a great many of the names in our western geography, it is interesting to know from official sources the principles which governed in this important work. Writing upon this point, Dr. Hayden says:*

"In attaching names to the many mountain peaks, new streams, and other geographical localities, the discovery of which falls to the pleasant lot of the explorer in the untrodden wilds of the West, I have followed the rigid law of priority, and given the one by which they have been generally known among the people of the country, whether whites or Indians; but if, as is often the case, no suitable descriptive name can be secured from the surroundings, a personal one may then be attached, and the names of eminent men who have identified themselves with the great cause, either in the fields of science or legislation, naturally rise first in the mind."

In the more recent and thorough survey of the Park by the United States Geological Survey, it became necessary to provide names for those subordinate features which, in a less restricted field, the early explorers had thought unworthy of notice. Professor Arnold Hague, upon whom this work has principally fallen, thus states the rule which he has followed:†

"In consultation with Mr. Henry Gannett, geologist in charge of geography, it was agreed that the necessary new names to designate the unnamed mountains, valleys, and streams should be mainly selected from the beasts, birds, fishes, trees, flowers, and minerals found within the Park or the adjacent country."

* F. V. Hayden, *Fifth Annual Report* (1871), 8.

† United States Geological Survey, *Annual Report for the Year Ending June 30, 1887* (Washington, Government Printing Office, 1887), I, 152.

The christening of the hot springs and geysers of the Park has been singularly fortunate. The names are in all cases characteristic. They are not studied efforts, but are simply the spontaneous utterances from first impressions by those who had never seen, and had heard but little of, similar phenomena. It is doubtful if the most careful study could improve them, and tourists will agree with General Poe who referred as follows to this subject when he visited the Park in 1877:*

"The region of these geysers has been rightly named Fire Hole, and one almost wonders that in this country, where the tendency is to name natural objects after men who have a temporary prominence, this interesting place and its assemblage of wonders should have so completely escaped, and in general and in particular received names so very appropriate."

In the race for the geographical honors of the Park, the prize fell neither to the United States Geological Survey nor even to Colonel Norris, though each was a close competitor. It was won by that mythical potentate of whose sulphurous empire this region is thought by some to be simply an outlying province. Starting with "Colter's Hell," the list grew until it contained "Hell Roaring Creek," "Hell Broth Springs," "Hell's Half Acre," "Satan's Arbor," and the Devil's "Den," "Workshop," "Kitchen," "Stairway," "Slide," "Caldron," "Punch Bowl," "Frying Pan," "Well," "Elbow," "Thumb," "Inkstand," etc., etc. It is some satisfaction to know that this rude and fiery nomenclature is gradually falling into disuse.

In a measure from sympathy with the purpose of the early name-givers, and to help those who take an interest in such matters to know when, by whom, and why the geographical names of the Park were given, . . . [a select] list of these names, with a few from adjacent territory, has been prepared. The letters and number immediately after the names . . . give marginal references on the map to facilitate identification. The date of christening and the name of the christening party next follow. When these cannot be determined with precision, the

* Generals P. H. Sheridan and W. T. Sherman, "Inspection Made in the Summer of 1877" (Washington, Government Printing Office, 1878), 79.

work is credited to the authors of the map upon which they first appear. Next comes whatever account is discoverable of the origin of the names, authority being quoted, as far as possible, from the writings of whoever bestowed them. . . . The abbreviation "U.S.G.S." is for "United States Geological Survey."*[1]

* The organization now known as the United States Geological Survey dates from 1879, when it superseded the various independent surveys which had previously been made under King, Wheeler, Powell, and Hayden. The Hayden surveys . . . are alone here considered of those prior to 1879.

[1] Names which Chittenden lists as "characteristic," which have no interesting history, are deleted from this revision. The *Haynes Guide* contains up-to-date place name identifications. What has been retained here are place names which have origins of historical or biographical interest.

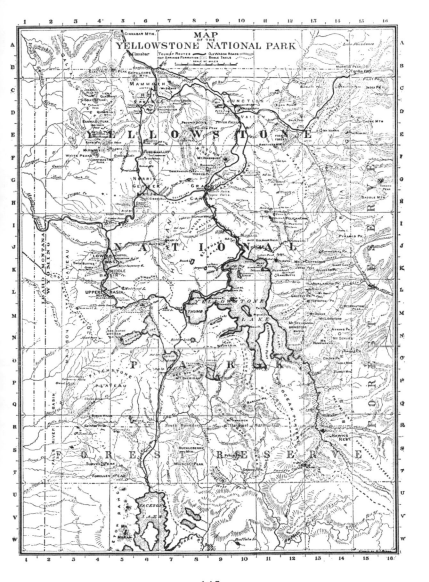

MAP
OF THE
YELLOWSTONE NATIONAL PARK

145

II

Mountain Ranges, Peaks, Buttes, Ridges, Hills

Abiathar Peak—C:14—1885—U.S.G.S.—For Charles *Abiathar* White, Paleontologist, U.S. Geological Survey.

Absaroka Range—A-X:12–16—1885—U.S.G.S.—This range of mountains has had an unfortunate christening history. It was first known as the Yellowstone Range, from its close relation to the Yellowstone River, of which it is the source. The original name dates from as far back as 1863, and was adopted by the first explorers of the Park country. It was officially recognized in 1871, by both the Corps of Engineers and the United States Geological Survey. When the Park was created this range became its real eastern boundary, and many of its peaks were named for those who had borne prominent parts in its history. The name had thus an added claim to perpetuity. It passed into general use, and appears in all the writings of the United States Geological Survey down to 1883.

In 1873, Captain W. A. Jones, of the Corps of Engineers, led an expedition through these mountains—the first that ever crossed them. He gave them a new name, "Sierra Shoshone." Except for the fact that he was violating the rule of priority, his action in giving this name, as well as his judgment in its selection, were of unquestionable propriety. It was a tribe of the Shoshonean family who alone dwelt in the Park, or among these mountains, and it was entirely fitting to commemorate this fact in a distinct and permanent manner. The name passed rapidly into public use, and by 1880 had practically supplanted the original name.

For reasons that can hardly be made to appear satisfactory,

the United States Geological Survey, in 1883, or soon after, rejected both these names and adopted in their place Absaroka, "the Indian name of the Crow nation" (Hague). Of course this action can have no pretense of justification from the standpoint of the "rigid law of priority." There are very few instances in American geography of a similar disregard for the rights of previous explorers. Unfortunately, not even the argument of appropriateness can be urged in its defense. These mountains, except that portion north of the Park, were never properly Crow territory, and the name is thus distinctly an importation. Its future use is now unhappily assured on account of its formal adoption (for reasons wholly inadequate, it is true,) by the United States Board on Geographical Names. Against the influence of the government, with its extensive series of publications, even though committed to the perpetuation of an error, it is idle to contend; but it is greatly to be deplored that a feature of the Park scenery of such commanding prominence should not bear a name at least remotely suggestive of some natural or historical association.

Atkins Peak—N:14—1885—U.S.G.S.—For John D. C. Atkins, Indian Commissioner, 1885–1888.

Bannock Peak—D:4—1885—U.S.G.S.—From the name of a tribe of Indians who inhabited the country to the southwest of the Park and were finally settled on a reservation in southern Idaho. What is known as the Great Bannock Trail, passed along the valley of Indian Creek, some distance south of this mountain. The spelling here given is that which custom seems finally to have settled upon; but *Bannack* would more nearly express the original pronunciation. The various spellings, some sixteen in number, come from the original *Panai'hti,* or *Bannai'hti,* meaning southern people.

Barlow Peak—Q:10—1895—U.S.G.S.—For Captain (now Colonel) J. W. Barlow, Corps of Engineers, U.S.A., leader of the military expedition which entered the Park region in 1871. His name was first applied to the upper course of the Snake River, but was recently transferred to a neighboring mountain peak.

147

Baronett Peak—C:13—1878—U.S.G.S.—For C. J. Baronett, "Yellowstone Jack," a famous scout and guide, closely connected with the history of the National Park, and builder of the first bridge across the Yellowstone River.

Baronett's career was adventurous beyond the average man of his class. He was born in Glencoe, Scotland, in 1829. His father was in the British naval service, and he early began to follow the sea. In his multitudinous wanderings we find him on the coast of Mexico during the Mexican War; on the Chinese coast in 1850, where he deserted his ship and fled to San Francisco; in 1852, in Australia after gold; the next year in Africa, still on a gold hunt; then in Australia again and in San Francisco; next in the Arctic seas as second mate on a whaling vessel; back in California in 1855; courier for Albert Sidney Johnston in the Mormon War; later in Colorado and California searching for gold; scout in the Confederate service until 1863; then in Mexico with the French under Maximilian, who made him a captain; back in California in 1864, and in Montana in September of the same year, where he at once set out on a prospecting trip which took him entirely through the region of the Yellowstone Park; later in the service of Gen. Custer as scout in the Indian territory; then in Mexico and finally back in Montana in 1870; finder of the lost Everts; builder of his celebrated bridge in 1871; in the Black Hills in 1875, where he slew a local editor who had unjustly reflected upon him in his paper; scout in the Sioux, Nez Percé, and Bannock Wars, 1876–78; Indian trader for many years; engaged in innumerable prospecting ventures; and still, at the age of sixty-six, searching with his old time ardor for the elusive yellow metal.

Bunsen Peak—D:6—1872—U.S.G.S.—For the eminent chemist and physicist, Robert Wilhelm Bunsen; inventor of the Bunsen electric cell and of the Bunsen gas burner; co-discoverer with Kirchoff of the principle of spectrum analysis; and the first thorough investigator of the phenomena of geyser action.

Chittenden, Mt.—K:12—1878—U.S.G.S.—"Of the prom-

148

inent peaks of this [the Absaroka] range may be mentioned Mount Chittenden, named for Mr. George B. Chittenden, whose name has long been identified with this survey."— Gannett.*

Cinnabar Mountain—A:5—Named prior to 1870.—"So named from the color of its rocks, which have been mistaken for Cinnabar, although the red color is due to iron."—Hayden. The Devil's Slide (also named before 1870) is on this mountain.

Colter Peak—O:13—1885—U.S.G.S.—For John Colter. (See Chapter III.)

Doane, Mt.—M:13—1870—Washburn Party—For Lieutenant Gustavus C. Doane, Second Cavalry, U.S. Army, commander of the military escort to the celebrated Washburn Expedition of 1870.

Lieutenant Doane was born in Illinois, May 29, 1840, and died in Bozeman, Mont., May 5, 1892. At the age of five he went with his parents, in wake of an ox team, to Oregon. In 1849 his family went to California at the outbreak of the gold excitement. He remained there ten years, in the meanwhile working his way through school. In 1862 he entered the Union service, went east with the California Hundred, and then joined a Massachusetts cavalry regiment. He was mustered out in 1865 as a first lieutenant. He joined the Carpet-baggers and is said to have become mayor of Yazoo City, Mississippi. He was appointed a Second Lieutenant in the Regular Army in 1868, and continued in the service until his death, attaining the rank of Captain.

Doane's whole career was actuated by a love of adventure. He had at various times planned a voyage to the polar regions or an expedition of discovery into Africa. But fate assigned him a middle ground, and he became prominently connected with the discovery of the Upper Yellowstone country. His part in the Expedition of 1870 is second to none. He made the first official report upon the wonders of the Yellowstone, and his fine descriptions have never been surpassed by any sub-

* F. V. Hayden, *Twelfth Annual Report,* 482.

sequent writer. Although suffering intense physical torture during the greater portion of the trip, it did not extinguish in him the truly poetic ardor with which those strange phenomena seem to have inspired him. Dr. Hayden says of this report: "I venture to state, as my opinion, that for graphic description and thrilling interest it has not been surpassed by any official report made to our government since the times of Lewis and Clark."[*]

Lieutenant Doane and Mr. Langford were the first white men known to have ascended any of the higher peaks of the Absaroka Range. From the summit of the mountain so ascended, Mr. Langford made the first known authentic sketch of Yellowstone Lake. This sketch was used soon after by General Washburn in compiling an official map of that section of country, and he was so much pleased with it that he named the mountain from which it was taken, Mt. Langford. At Mr. Langford's request, he named a neighboring peak, Mt. Doane.

Dunraven Peak—F : 9—1878—U.S.G.S.—"This I have named Dunraven Peak in honor of the Earl of Dunraven, whose travels and writings have done so much toward making this region known to our cousins across the water."—Gannett.[†]

Dunraven visited the Park in 1874. In 1876, he published his *Great Divide,* describing his travels in the West. The irrepressible Colonel Norris named this peak after himself, and coupled it with Mt. Washburn in a characteristic poem. But the United States Geological Survey decided otherwise, and transferred the Colonel's name to the north-east corner of the Park. (See *Mt. Norris.*)

Electric Peak—B:4–5—1872—U.S.G.S.—From the following circumstances, described by Mr. Henry Gannett, who ascended the mountain with surveying instruments, July 26, 1872:[‡]

"A thunder-shower was approaching as we neared the sum-

[*] F. V. Hayden, *Fifth Annual Report,* 8.
[†] F. V. Hayden, *Twelfth Annual Report,* 478.
[‡] F. V. Hayden, *Sixth Annual Report,* 807.

mit of the mountain. I was above the others of the party, and, when about fifty feet below the summit, the electric current began to pass through my body. At first I felt nothing, but heard a crackling noise, similar to a rapid discharge of sparks from a friction machine. Immediately after, I began to feel a tingling or prickling sensation in my head and the ends of my fingers, which, as well as the noise, increased rapidly, until, when I reached the top, the noise, which had not changed its character, was deafening, and my hair stood completely on end, while the tingling, pricking sensation was absolutely painful. Taking off my hat partially relieved it. I started down again, and met the others twenty-five or thirty feet below the summit. They were affected similarly, but in a less degree. One of them attempted to go to the top, but had proceeded but a few feet when he received quite a severe shock, which felled him as if he had stumbled. We then returned down the mountain about three hundred feet, and to this point we still heard and felt the electricity."

Elephant Back—J : 9—1871—U. S. G. S.—Characteristic. "On account of the almost vertical sides of this mountain, and the rounded form of the summit, it has received the name of the Elephant's Back."—Hayden.*

This name, as now applied, refers to a different feature from that originally designated by it. Many years before the Park was discovered, it was used to denote the long ridge of which Mt. Washburn is the commanding summit, and which was distinctly visible from beyond the present limits of the Park, both north and south. It so appears upon Raynolds' map of 1860, and was so used by the Washburn Expedition (1870), by Captain Barlow (1871), and by Captain Jones (1873). The United States Geological Survey, however, in 1871, transferred the name to an inconspicuous ridge more than a thousand feet lower than the surrounding mountains. Whether the change was made by accident or design does not appear. Captain Ludlow, as late as 1875, refers to it and deplores the fact that it had taken place.

* F. V. Hayden, *Fifth Annual Report*, 98.

Everts, Mt.—C:7—1870—Washburn Party—For Hon. Truman C. Everts, member of the Expedition of 1870, whose terrible experience is elsewhere alluded to. The following succinct account is from the pen of Lieutenant Doane, and is in the main correct:*

"On the first day of his absence, he had left his horse standing unfastened, with all his arms and equipments strapped upon his saddle; the animal became frightened, ran away into the woods, and he was left without even a pocket knife as a means of defense. Being very near-sighted, and totally unused to traveling in a wild country without guides, he became completely bewildered. He wandered down to the Snake River Lake [Hart Lake], where he remained twelve days, sleeping near the hot springs to keep from freezing at night, and climbing to the summits each day in the endeavor to trace out his proper course. Here he subsisted on thistle-roots, boiled in the springs, and was kept up a tree the greater part of one night by a California lion. After gathering and cooking a supply of thistle-roots, he managed to strike the south-west point of the [Yellowstone] Lake, and followed around the north side to the Yellowstone [River], finally reaching our [old] camp opposite the Grand Cañon: He was twelve days out before he thought to kindle a fire by using the lenses of his field glass, but after ward carried a burning brand with him in all his wanderings. Herds of game passed by him during the night, on many occasions when he was on the verge of starvation. In addition to a tolerable supply of thistle-roots, he had nothing for over thirty days but a handful of minnows and a couple of snow-birds. Twice he went five days without food, and three days without water, in that country which is a net-work of streams and springs. He was found on the verge of the great plateau, above the mouth of Gardiner's River. A heavy snow-storm had extinguished his fire; his supply of thistle-roots was exhausted; he was partially deranged, and perishing with cold. A large lion was killed near him, on the trail, which he said had followed

* Lieutenant Gustavus C. Doane, *Report upon the Yellowstone Expedition of 1870,* 37.

him at a short distance for several days previously. It was a miraculous escape, considering the utter helplessness of the man, lost in a forest wilderness, and with the storms of winter at hand."

On the thirty-seventh day of his wanderings (September 9 to October 16), he was discovered by Jack Baronett and George A. Pritchett, near the great trail on a high mountain a few miles west of Yancey's. Baronett threw up a mound of stones to mark the spot. He carried Everts in his arms the rest of that day, and passed the night on a small tributary of Black-tail Deer Creek. The next day he was taken on a saddle to near the mouth of the Gardiner.

The commemoration of this adventure in the naming of Mt. Everts was an awkward mischance. The mountain which should bear the name is Mt. Sheridan. It was named for Everts by the Washburn Party the night before he was lost, in recognition of his having been the first white man (except Mr. Hedges, who was with him) known to have visited its summit. In the writings of the Washburn Party after their return, it is so used; one very interesting article, by Mr. Hedges, with this name as a title, being published in the *Helena Herald* before it was known that Mr. Everts had been found. But the name, Mt. Everts, was finally given to the broad plateau between the Gardiner and the Yellowstone, a feature which is not a mountain at all, and which is ten miles from where Everts was found. The actual locality of the finding was erroneously supposed to be near "Rescue Creek."

In 1871, Captain Barlow ascended the mountain which should have borne the name of Everts, and called it Mt. Sheridan, in ignorance of its former christening.

Factory Hill—O:8—1885—U.S.G.S.—The term "factory" has at various times been applied to several different localities in the Park because of their striking resemblance on frosty mornings to an active factory town. The resemblance was noted as far back as 1829. The name has now become fixed, as above indicated.

Flat Mountain—N:9—1871—U.S.G.S.—Characteristic.—

This mountain had already been named by the Washburn Party Yellow Mountain, from its color.

Folsom Peak—E:8—1895—U.S.G.S.—For David E. Folsom, leader of the Expedition of 1869, and author of the first general description of the valley of the Upper Yellowstone.

Forellen Peak—T:5—1885—U.S.G.S.—From the German name for trout.

Gallatin Range—A-F:1–4—Name in use prior to 1870. Raynolds has "Mt. Gallatin" on his map. Gallatin River (see name) rises in this range.

Hancock, Mt.—R:10—1871—Barlow—For General W. S. Hancock, U.S. Army, who, as commanding officer of the Department of Dakota, had lent his active aid in the prosecution of the Yellowstone explorations.

Hedges Peak—G:9—1895—U.S.G.S.—For Cornelius Hedges, a prominent member of the Washburn Expedition, author of a series of descriptive articles upon the trip, and first to advance and publicly advocate the idea of setting apart that region as a National Park.

Holmes, Mt.—F:4—1878—U.S.G.S.—For W. F. Holmes, Geologist, U.S. Geological Survey. This peak had been previously called Mt. Madison.

Hoyt, Mt.—L:13—1881—Norris—For the Hon. John W. Hoyt, then governor of Wyoming.

Humphreys, Mt.—N:14—1871—Barlow—For General A. A. Humphreys, then Chief of Engineers, U.S.A.

Index Peak—G:16—This mountain, and Pilot Knob near it, received their names from unknown sources prior to 1870.

"One of them [the peaks] derives its name from its shape, like a closed hand with the index-finger extending upward, while the other is visible from so great a distance on every side that it forms an excellent landmark for the wandering miner, and thus it appropriate name of Pilot Knob."—Hayden.*

Joseph Peak—C:4—1885—U.S.G.S.—For Chief Joseph, the famous Nez Percé leader in the war of 1877. He deservedly ranks among the most noted of the North American Indians.

* F. V. Hayden, *Sixth Annual Report,* 48.

His remarkable conduct of the campaign of 1877 and his uniform abstinence from those barbarous practices which have always characterized Indian warfare were a marvel to all who were familiar with the facts. No Indian chief ever commanded to such a degree the respect and even friendship of his enemies.

Junction Butte—D:10—When or by whom given not known. The name arose, of course, from the fact that this butte stands at the junction of the two important streams, the Yellowstone and Lamar rivers. Barlow records that the Butte was known as "Square Butte" at the time of his visit in 1871.

Langford, Mt.—M:13—1870—Washburn Party—For the Hon. Nathaniel Pitt Langford, first superintendent of the Yellowstone National Park.

Mr. Langford was born August 9, 1832, in Westmoreland, Oncida County, New York. His early life was spent on his father's farm, and his education was obtained by winter attendance at district school. At nineteen, he became clerk in the Oneida Bank of Utica. In 1854, he went to St. Paul, where we find him, in 1855, cashier of the banking house of Marshall & Co., and in 1858, cashier of the Bank of the State of Minnesota. In 1862, he went to Montana as second in command of the Northern Overland Expedition, consisting of 130 men and 53 wagons drawn by oxen. In 1864, he was made Collector of Internal Revenue for the new territory. In 1868, he was appointed by President Johnson Governor of Montana, but as this was after the Senate's imbroglio with the President and its refusal to confirm any more presidential appointments, he did not reach this office. He was one of the famous Montana Vigilantes, a member of the Yellowstone Expedition of 1870, and first Superintendent of the newly created Park. In 1872, he was appointed National Bank Examiner for the Pacific States and Territories, and held the office for thirteen years. He now resides in St. Paul, Minnesota. He is author of a series of articles in *Scribner's* for 1871, describing the newly-discovered wonders of the Yellowstone, and of the important work, *Vigilante Days and Ways,* the most complete history in existence of that critical period in Montana history.

155

The notable part which Mr. Langford bore in the discovery of the Upper Yellowstone country, and in the creation of the Yellowstone National Park, has been fully set forth elsewhere. He has always been its ardent friend, and his enthusiasm upon the subject in the earlier days of its history drew upon him the mild raillery of his friends, who were wont to call him "National Park" Langford—a sobriquet to which the initials of his real name readily lent themselves.

For the circumstance of naming Mt. Langford, see "Mt. Doane."

Mary Mountain—J:7—Probably so named by tourists from Mary Lake, which rests on the summit.

Moran, Mt.—W:5—1872—U.S.G.S.—For the artist, Thomas Moran, who produced the picture of the Grand Cañon now in the Capitol at Washington.

Norris, Mt.—E:13—1878—U.S.G.S.—For Philetus W. Norris, second superintendent of the Park, and the most conspicuous figure in its history.

He was born at Palmyra, New York, August 17, 1821. At the age of eight, he was tourist guide at Portage Falls on the Genesee River, New York, and at seventeen he was in Manitoba in the service of British fur traders. In 1842, he settled in Williams County, Ohio, where he founded the village of Pioneer. Between 1850 and 1860 he visited the Far West. At the outbreak of the Civil War, he entered the army and served a short time as spy and captain of scouts. He was then placed in charge of Rebel prisoners on Johnson's Island. He next entered politics as member of the Ohio House of Representatives, but being later defeated for the State Senate, he joined the United States Sanitary Commission and went again to the front. He soon returned and became trustee of certain landed property near the city of Detroit belonging to officers and soldiers of both armies. These lands he reclaimed at great expense from their original swampy condition, and built thereon the village of Norris, now part of Detroit. In 1870, he went west again and undertook to enter the Park region in June of that year, but permitted the swollen condition of the streams to defeat his project. He thus missed the honor which a few months later fell to the Washburn Party—a misfortune which he never ceased to deplore. In 1875, he again visited the Park, and in 1877, became its second superintendent. In 1882, he returned to Detroit, after which he was employed by the government to explore old Indian mounds, forts, villages, and tombs, and to collect relics for the National Museum. He died at Rocky Hill, Kentucky, January 14, 1885. He is author of the following works: five annual reports as superintendent of the Park; *The Calumet of the Coteau,* a volume of verse, with much additional matter relating to the Park; and a long series of articles on "The Great West," published in the *Norris Suburban* in 1876–78.

The above sketch sufficiently discloses the salient characteristic of Norris' career. His life was that of the pioneer, and was spent in dealing first blows in the subjugation of a primeval wilderness. He was "blazing trails," literally and figuratively, all his days, leaving to others the building of the finished highway. It is therefore not surprising that his work lacks the element of completeness, which comes only from patient attention to details. Nowhere is this defect more apparent than in his writings. A distinct literary talent, and something of the poet's inspiration, were, to use his own words, "well nigh strangled" by the "stern realities of border life." His prose abounds in aggregations of more than one hundred words between periods, so ill arranged and barbarously punctuated as utterly to bewilder the reader. His verse—we have searched in vain for a single quatrain that would justify reproduction. Nevertheless, his writings, like his works, were always to some good purpose. They contained much useful information, and, being widely read throughout the West, had a large and beneficial influence.

Perhaps no better or more generous estimate of his character can be found than in the following words of Mr. Langford, who knew him well: "He was a good man, a true man, faithful to his friends, of every kind heart, grateful for kindnesses, of more than ordinary personal courage, rather vain of his poetical genius, and fond of perpetuating his name in prominent features of scenery."

Concerning which last characteristic it may be noted that three mountain peaks, one geyser basin, one pass, and an uncertain number of other features of the Park, were thought by Colonel Norris deserving of this distinction. With inimitable fidelity to this trait of his character, he had even selected as his final resting-place the beautiful open glade on the south side of the Grand Cañon, just below the Lower Falls.

Pilot Knob—See *Index Peak*.

Roaring Mountain—F:6—1885—U.S.G.S.—"It takes its name from the shrill, penetrating sound of the steam constantly escaping from one or more vents near the summit."—Hague.

Schurz, Mt.—N:14—1885—U.S.G.S.—For Carl Schurz, Secretary of the Interior during President Hayes's administration. This name was first given by Colonel Norris to the prominent ridge on the west side of the Gibbon Cañon.

Sepulcher Mountain—B-C:5-6—The origin of this name is unknown. The following remarks concerning it are from the pen of Prof. Wm. H. Holmes:*

"Why this mountain received such a melancholy appellation I have not been able to discover. So far as I know, the most important thing buried beneath its dark mass is the secret of its structure. It is possible that the form suggested the name."

Sheepeater Cliffs—D:7—1879—Norris—From the name of a tribe of Indians, the only known aboriginal occupants of what is now the Yellowstone Park. It was upon one of the "ancient and but recently deserted, secluded, unknown haunts" of these Indians, that Colonel Norris, "in rapt astonishment," stumbled one day, and was so impressed by what he saw, that he gave the neighboring cliff its present name. He thus describes this retreat:†

"It is mainly carpeted with soft grass, dotted, fringed, and overhung with small pines, firs and cedars, and, with the sub-

---

* F. V. Hayden, *Twelfth Annual Report*, 15.
† *Annual Report of Superintendent of the Park for 1879*, 10.

dued and mingled murmur of the rapids and cataracts above and below it, and the laughing ripple of the gliding stream, is truly an enchanting dell—a wind and storm sheltered refuge for the feeble remnant of a fading race."

Sheridan, Mt.—P : 8—1871—Barlow—For Gen. P. H. Sheridan, who actively forwarded all the early exploring expeditions in this region, and, at a later day, twice visited the Park. His public warnings at this time of the danger to which the Park was exposed from vandals, poachers, and railroad promoters and his vigorous appeal for its protection had great influence in bringing about a more efficient and enlightened policy in regard to that reservation. (See *Mt. Everts.*)

Signal Hills—M : 12—1871—U.S.G.S.—A ridge extending back from Signal Point on the Yellowstone Lake.

Stevenson, Mt.—M : 13—1871—U.S.G.S.—For James Stevenson, long prominently connected with the U.S. Geological Survey.

"In honor of his great services not only during the past season, but for over twelve years of unremitting toil as my assistant, oftentimes without pecuniary reward, and with but little of the scientific recognition that usually comes to the original explorer, I have desired that one of the principal islands of the lake and one of the noble peaks reflected in its clear waters should bear his name forever."—Hayden.*

Mr. Stevenson was born in Maysville, Ky., December 24, 1840. He early displayed a taste for exploration and natural history, and such reading as his limited education permitted was devoted to books treating of these subjects. At the age of thirteen he ran away from home and joined a party of Hudson's Bay Fur Company's traders, bound up the Missouri River. On the same boat was Dr. F. V. Hayden, then on his way to explore the fossiliferous region of the Upper Missouri and Yellowstone rivers. Noticing Stevenson's taste for natural history, he invited him to join him in his work. Stevenson accepted; and thus began a relation which continued for more than a quarter of a century, and which gave direction to the rest of his life.

* F. V. Hayden, *Fifth Annual Report*, 5.

He was engaged in several explorations between 1850 and 1860, connected with the Pacific railroad surveys, and with others under Lieutenants G. K. Warren and W. F. Raynolds. In 1861 he entered the Union service as a private soldier, and left it in 1865 with an officer's commission. After the war he resumed his connection with Dr. Hayden. He was mainly instrumental in the organization of the United States Geological Survey of the Territories in 1867, and during the next twelve years he was constantly engaged in promoting its welfare. When the consolidation of the various geographical and geological surveys took place in 1879, under the name of the United States Geological Survey, he became associated with the United States Bureau of Ethnology. He had always shown a taste for ethnological investigations and his scientific work during the rest of his life was in this direction, principally among the races of New Mexico and Arizona. He died in New York City July 25, 1888.

In the paragraph quoted above from Dr. Hayden there is more than any but the few who are familiar with the early history of the geological surveys will understand. It rarely happens that a master is so far indebted to a servant for his success, as was true of the relation of Dr. Hayden and James Stevenson. Stevenson's great talent lay in the organization and management of men. His administrative ability in the field was invaluable to the Survey of which Hayden was chief, and his extraordinary influence with congressmen was a vital element in its early growth. His part in the Yellowstone explorations of 1871 and 1872 is second to none in importance. It will not be forgotten that he was the first to build and launch a boat upon the Yellowstone Lake, nor that he, and Mr. Langford who was with him, were the first white men to reach the summit of the Grand Teton.

Survey Peak—T:4—1885—U.S.G.S.—This mountain was a prominent signaling point for the Indians. It was first named Monument Peak by Richard Leigh, who built a stone mound on its summit.

Teton, Grand—Not on Map—This mountain has borne its

present name for upward of four score years. Through more than half a century it was a cynosure to the wandering trapper, miner, and explorer. The name has passed into all the literature of that period, which will ever remain one of the most fascinating in our western history. Indeed, it has become the classic designation of the most interesting historic summit of the Rocky Mountains. That it should always retain this designation in memory of the nameless pioneers who have been guided by it across the wilderness, and thousands of whom have perished beneath its shadow, would seem to be a self-evident proposition. Individual merit, no matter how great, can never justify the usurpation of its place by any personal name whatever. An attempt to do this was made in 1872 by the United States Geological Survey, who rechristened it Mt. Hayden. The new name has never gained any local standing, and although it has crept into many maps its continued use ought to be discouraged. It is greatly to the credit of Dr. Hayden that he personally disapproved the change, so far at least, as very rarely, if ever, to refer to the mountain by its new name.

Three Rivers Peak—E:4—1885—U.S.G.S.—Branches of the Madison, Gallatin, and Gardiner rivers take their rise from its slopes.

Thunderer, The—D:14—1885—U.S.G.S.—Seemingly a great focus for thunder storms.

Washburn, Mt.—F:9—1870—Washburn Party—For General Henry Dana Washburn, chief of the Yellowstone Expedition of 1870.

General Washburn was born in Windsor, Vt., March 28, 1832. His parents moved to Ohio during his infancy. He received a common school education and at fourteen began teaching school. He entered Oberlin College, but did not complete his course. At eighteen he went to Indiana where he resumed school-teaching. At twenty-one he entered the New York State and National Law School, from which he graduated. At twenty-three he was elected auditor of Vermilion County, Indiana.

His war record was a highly honorable one. He entered the

army as private in 1861 and left it as brevet brigadier-general in 1865. His service was mainly identified with the Eighteenth Indiana, of which he became colonel. He was in several of the western campaigns, notably in that of Vicksburg, in which he bore a prominent part. In the last year of the war he was with Sherman's army, and for a short time after its close was in command of a military district in southern Georgia. In 1864, he was elected to Congress over the Hon. Daniel W. Voorhees, and again, in 1866, over the Hon. Solomon W. Claypool. At the expiration of his second term, he was appointed by President Grant surveyor-general of Montana, which office he held until his death.

It was during his residence in Montana that the famous Yellowstone Expedition of 1870 took place. His part in that important work is perhaps the most notable feature of his career. As leader of the expedition he won the admiration and affection of its members. He was the first to send to Washington specimens from the geyser formations. He ardently espoused the project of setting apart this region as a public park and was on his way to Washington in its interest when his career was cut short by death. The hardship and exposure of the expedition had precipitated the catastrophe to which he had long been tending. He left Helena in November, 1870, and died of consumption at his home in Clinton, Indiana, January 26, 1871.

General Washburn's name was given to this mountain by a unanimous vote of the party on the evening of August 28, 1870, as a result of the following incident related by Mr. Langford:

"Our first Sunday in camp was at Tower Creek. The forest around us was very dense, and we were somewhat at a loss in deciding what course we needed to follow in order to reach Yellowstone Lake. We had that day crossed a *fresh* Indian trail, a circumstance which admonished us of the necessity of watchfulness so as to avoid disaster. While we were resting in camp, General Washburn, without our knowledge and unattended, made his way to the mountain, from the summit of which, overlooking the dense forest which environed us, he saw Yellowstone Lake, our objective point, and carefully noted its direction from our camp. This intelligence was most joyfully received by us, for it relieved our minds of all anxiety concerning our course of travel and dispelled the fears of some of our party lest we should become inextricably involved in that wooded labyrinth."

Yount Peak—Not on map—1878—U.S.G.S.—Source of the Yellowstone—Named for an old trapper and guide of that region.

III

Streams

[Map locations refer only to outlets, or to points where streams pass off the limits of the map.]

Alum Creek—H:9—Name known prior to 1870—Characteristic.

Amethyst Creek—E:12—1878—U.S.G.S.—Flows from Amethyst Mountain.

Amphitheater Creek—D:13—1885—U.S.G.S.—From form of valley near its mouth.

Atlantic Creek—S:13—1873—Jones—Flows from Two-Ocean Pass down the Atlantic slope.

Bear Creek—B:7—1863—Party of prospectors under one Austin. "On the way they found fair prospects in a creek on the east side of the Yellowstone, and finding also a hairless cub, called the gulch "Bear."—Topping.

Bechler River—R:1—1872—U.S.G.S.—For Gustavus R. Bechler, topographer on the Snake River Division of the Hayden Expedition of 1872.

Black-tail Deer Creek—B:8—Named prior to 1870—Characteristic.

Boone Creek—T:1—Named prior to 1870—For Robert Withrow, an eccentric pioneer of Irish descent, who used to call himself "Daniel Boone the Second."

Bridge Creek—K:9—1871—U.S.G.S.—Characteristic.

At one point, soon after leaving camp, we found a most singular natural bridge of the trachyte, which gives passage to a small stream, which we called Bridge Creek."—Hayden.

"Natural Bridge" is really over a branch of Bridge Creek.

Cache Creek—F:13—1863—Prospecting party under one Austin were in camp on this stream when they were surprised by Indians and all their stock stolen except one or two mules. Being unable to carry all their baggage from this point, they *cached* what they could not place on the mules, or could not themselves carry. From this circumstance arose the name.

Calfee Creek—F:13—1880—Norris—For H. B. Calfee, a photographer of note.

"Some seven miles above Cache Creek we passed the mouth of another stream in a deep, narrow, timbered valley, which we named Calfee Creek, after the famous photographer of the Park. Five miles further on, we reached the creek which Miller recognized as the one he descended in retreating from the Indians in 1870, and which, on this account, we called Miller's Creek."—Norris.*

Conant Creek—T:1—Prior to 1870—By Richard Leigh for one Al Conant, who went to the mountains in 1865, and who came near losing his life on this stream.

Coulter Creek—R:8—1885—U.S.G.S.—For John M. Coulter, botanist in the Hayden Expedition of 1872.

Crevice Creek—C:7—1867—Prospecting party under one Lou Anderson.

"They found gold in a crevice at the mouth of the first stream above Bear, and named it, in consequence, Crevice Gulch. Hubbel went ahead the next day for a hunt, and upon his return he was asked what kind of a stream the next creek was. 'It's a hell roarer,' was his reply, and Hell Roaring is its name to this day. The second day after this, he was again ahead, and, the same question being asked him, he said: ' 'T was but a slough.' When the party came to it, they found a rushing torrent, and, in crossing, a pack horse and his load were swept away, but the name of Slough Creek remains."—Topping.

De Lacy Creek—M:6—1880—Norris—For Walter W. De Lacy, first white man known to have passed along the valley. (See *Shoshone Lake*.) First named Madison Creek by the Hayden party in 1871.

* *Annual Report of the Superintendent of the Park for 1880, 7.*

165

Firehole River—I:4—This name and "Burnt Hole" have been used to designate the geyser basins and the stream flowing through them since at least as far back at 1830. Captain Bonneville says it was well known to his men. The term "Hole" is a relic of the early days when the open valleys or parks among the mountains were called "holes." The descriptive "fire, naturally arose from the peculiar character of that region."

Firehole, Little—L:4—1878—U.S.G.S.—From main stream.

Gallatin River—A:1—1805—Lewis and Clark—For Albert Gallatin, Secretary of Treasury under President Jefferson.

Gardiner River—B:6—This name, which, after "Yellowstone," is the most familiar and important name in the Park, is the most difficult to account for. The first authentic use of the name occurs in 1870, in the writings of the Washburn party. In Mr. Langford's journal, kept during the expedition, is the following entry for August 25, 1870: "At nineteen miles from our morning camp we came to Gardiner River, at the mouth of which we camped." As the party did not originate the name, and as they make no special reference to it in any of their writings, it seems clear that it must already have been known to them at the time of their arrival at the stream. None of the surviving members has the least recollection concerning it. The stream had been known to prospectors during the preceding few years as Warm Spring Creek, and the many "old timers" consulted on the subject erroneously think that the present name was given by the Washburn Party or by the Hayden Party of 1871. What is its real origin is therefore a good deal of a mystery.

The only clue, and that not a satisfactory one, which has come under our observation is to be found in the book *River of the West,* already quoted. Reference is there made to a trapper by the name of Gardiner, who lived in the Upper Yellowstone country as far back as 1830 and was at one time a companion of Joseph Meek, the hero of the book. In another place it is stated that in 1838, Meek started alone from Missouri Lake (probably Red Rock Lake) "for the Gallatin Fork of the Missouri, trapping in a mountain basin called Gardiner's Hole. . . . On his return, in another basin called Burnt Hole, he found a buffalo skull, etc." As is well known, the sources of the Gallatin and Gardiner are interlaced with each other, and this reference strongly points to the present Gardiner Valley as "Gardiner's Hole." The route across the Gallatin Range to Mammoth Hot Springs, and thence back by way of the Fire-hole Basin, was doubtless a natural one then as it is now. It is therefore reasonable to suppose that this name came from an old hunter in the early years of the century, and that the Wash-burn Party received it from some surviving descendant of those times.

Gibbon River—I : 4—1872—U. S. G. S.—For Gen. John Gibbon, U.S.A., who first explored it.

"We have named this stream in honor of Gen. John Gibbon, United States Army, who has been in military command of Montana for some years, and has, on many occasions, rendered the survey most important services."—Hayden.*

Hell Roaring Creek—C : 9—1867—See *Crevice Creek*.

Indian Creek—E:6—1878—U.S.G.S.—See *Bannock Peak*.

Jones Creek—K:15—1880—Norris—For Captain (now Lieutenant-Colonel) W. A. Jones, Corps of Engineers, U.S.A., who first explored it. Captain Jones was leader of an important expedition through the Park in 1873, and has since been largely identified with the development of the Park road system.

Lamar River—D:10—1885—U.S.G.S.—For the Hon. L. Q. C. Lamar, Secretary of the Interior during the first administration of President Cleveland. The stream is locally known only by its original designation, the "East Fork of the Yellowstone."

Lewis River—R:7—1872—U.S.G.S.—From *Lewis Lake*, which see.

Madison River—G : 1—1805—Lewis and Clark—For James Madison, Secretary of State to Thomas Jefferson.

Mason Creek—L : 16—1881—Norris—For Major Julius W. Mason, U.S.A., commander of escort to Gov. Hoyt, of

* F. V. Hayden, *Sixth Annual Report,* 55.

Wyoming, on the latter's reconnaissance for a wagon road to the Park in 1881.

Miller Creek—G:13—1880—Norris—For a mountaineer named Miller. See *Calfee Creek*.

Nez Percé Creek—J:4—1878—U.S.G.S.—The Nez Percé Indians passed up this stream on their raid through the Park in 1877. It had previously been called "East Fork of the Firehole." Prof. Bradley, of the U.S. Geological Survey, christened it Hayden's Fork in 1872. (See Chapter XIII, Part I.)

Pacific Creek—W:11—1873—Jones—Flows from Two-Ocean Pass down the Pacific slope.

Pelican Creek—K:10—Probably named by the Washburn Party in 1870. Hayden and Barlow, in 1871, use the name as though it were already a fixture. Mr. Hedges says of this stream:

"About the mouth of the little stream that we had just crossed were numerous shallows and bars, which were covered by the acre with ducks, geese, huge white-breasted cranes, and long-beaked pelicans, while the solitary albatross, or sea-gull, circled above our heads with a saucy look that drew many a random shot, and cost one, at least, its life."

Rescue Creek—C:7—1878—U.S.G.S.—Where Everts was *not* found. (See *Mt. Everts*.)

Sentinel Creek—J:4—1872—U.S.G.S.—"The two central ones [geyser mounds] are the highest, and appear so much as if they were guarding the Upper Valley, that this stream was called Sentinel Branch."—Bradley.

Snake River—W:8—1805—Lewis and Clark—From the Snake or Shoshone Indians, who dwelt in its valley.

Soda Butte Creek—E:12—Probably named by miners prior to 1870. From an extinct geyser or hot spring cone near the mouth of the stream.

Solution Creek—M:8—1885—U.S.G.S.—The outlet of *Riddle* Lake.

Stinkingwater River—L:16—1807—John Colter—From an offensive hot spring near the junction of the principal forks of the stream. A most interesting fact, to which attention was first publicly called by Prof. Arnold Hague, is the occurrence on the map, which Lewis and Clark sent to President Jefferson in the spring of 1805, of the name "Stinking Cabin Creek," very nearly in the locality of the river Stinkingwater. Prof. Hague, who published an interesting paper concerning this map in *Science* for November 4, 1877, thinks that possibly some trapper had penetrated this region even before 1804. But with Lewis and Clark's repeated statements that no white man had reached the Yellowstone prior to 1805, it seems more likely that the name was derived from the Indians. [Now known as the Shoshone.—ed.]

Sulphur Creek—G : 9—1878—U. S. G. S.—Characteristic. —Locally this name is applied to a stream which flows from the hot springs at the base of Sulphur Mountain.

Surprise Creek—P : 9—1885—U. S. G. S.—Its course, as made known by recent explorations, was surprisingly different from that which earlier explorations had indicated.

Tangled Creek—J:4—1885—U.S.G.S.—Characteristic.— A hot water stream which flows in numberless interlaced channels.

Thoroughfare Creek—R: 13—1885—U. S. G. S.—Its valley forms part of a very practicable route across the Yellowstone Range.

Tower Creek—D : 10—1870—Washburn Party—From *Tower Falls,* which see.

Trail Creek—O : 12—1873—Jones—From an elk trail along it.

Trappers' Creek—P:13—1885—U.S.G.S.—A great beaver resort.

Violet Creek—I : 8—1872—U. S. G. S.—Characteristic.— "We named the small stream Violet Creek, from the profusion of violets growing upon its banks."—Peale.

Witch Creek—O:8—1878—U.S.G.S.— Probably from the prevalence of hot springs phenomena along its entire course.

Yellowstone River—U:16 (enters map); A:5 (leaves map). —See Part I, Chapter I.

IV

Water-Falls

Crystal Falls—G:8—1870—Washburn Party—Characteristic.—The total falls includes three cascades.

Firehole Falls—I:4—Takes name from river.

Kepler Cascade—L:5—1881—Norris.—For the son of Hon. John W. Hoyt, Ex-Governor of Wyoming, who accompanied his father on a reconnaissance for a wagon road to the Park in 1881. Norris speaks of him as "an intrepid twelve-year old" boy who "unflinchingly shared in all the hardships, privations, and dangers of the explorations of his father," which included many hundred miles of travel on horseback through that difficult country; and in admiration for the lad's pluck, he named this cascade in his honor.

Rainbow Falls—R:4—1885—U.S.G.S.—Characteristic—Total of three falls.

Tower Falls—D:10—1870—Washburn Party—Characteristic.

"By a vote of a majority of the party this fall was called Tower Fall."—Washburn.

"At the crest of the fall the stream has cut its way through amygdaloid masses, leaving tall spires of rock from 50 to 100 feet in height, and worn in every conceivable shape. . . . Several of them stand like sentinels on the very brink of the fall."—Doane.

Virginia Cascade—H:17—1886—By E. Lamartine, at that time foreman in charge of government work in Park.—For the wife of the Hon. Chas. Gibson, President of the Yellowstone Park Association.

Yellowstone Falls—H:9—From the river which flows over them.*

   * Record of the various measurements of the Upper and Lower Falls of the Yellowstone River.

   Folsom (1869) Upper Fall, 115 feet. Method not stated.
      Lower Fall, 350 feet. Line.
   Doane (1870) Upper Fall, 115 feet. Line.
   Langford (1870) Lower Fall, 350 feet. Line stretched on an incline.
   Moore's Sketch (1870) Lower Fall, 365 feet. Method not stated.
   Hayden (1871) Upper Fall, 140 feet. Method not stated.
      Lower Fall, 350 feet. Method not stated.
   Gannett (1872) Upper Fall, 140 feet. Barometer.
      Lower Fall, 395 feet. Comparison of angles subtended by Falls and by a tree of known height.
   Jones (1873) Upper Fall, 150 feet. Barometer.
      Lower Fall, 329 feet. Barometer.
   Ludlow (1875) Upper Fall, 110 feet. Line.
      Lower Fall, 310 feet. Line.
   Gannett (1878) Upper Fall, 112 feet. Line.
      Lower Fall, 297 feet. Line stretched on an incline.
   U.S.G.S. (Recent) Upper Fall, 109 feet. Method not stated.
      Lower Fall, 308 feet. Method not stated.
   Chittenden (1892) Upper Fall, 112 feet between point of first descent and level of pool below. Measured by means of a transit instrument. Width of gorge at brink of fall, and a few feet above water surface, 48 feet.

V

Lakes

Bridger Lake—R:13—Name a fixture prior to 1870.—For James Bridger, the Daniel Boone of the Rockies, and one of the most remarkable products of the trapping and gold-seeking eras.

He was born in Richmond, Va., in March, 1804, and died in Washington, Jackson Co., Mo., July 17, 1881. He must have gone west at a very early age for he is known to have been in the mountains in 1820. *Niles Register* for 1822 speaks of him as associated with Fitzpatrick in the Rocky Mountain Fur Company. Another record of this period reveals him as leader of a band of whites sent to retake stolen horses from the hostile Bannocks. In 1832, he had become a resident partner in the Rocky Mountain Fur Company. That he was a recognized leader among the early mountaineers while yet in his minority seems beyond question. He became "The Old Man of the Mountains" before he was thirty years of age.

Among the more prominent achievements of Bridger's life may be noted the following: He was long a leading spirit in the great Rocky Mountain Fur Company. He discovered Great Salt Lake and the noted Pass that bears his name. He built Fort Bridger in the lovely valley of Black Fork of Green River, where transpired many thrilling events connected with the history of the Mormons and "Forty-niners." He had explored, and could accurately describe, the wonders of the Yellowstone fully a quarter of a century before their final discovery.

In person he was tall and spare, straight and agile, eyes gray, hair brown and long, and abundant even in old age; expression mild, and manners agreeable. He was hospitable and generous and was always trusted and respected. He possessed to a high degree the confidence of the Indians, one of whom, a Shoshone woman, he made his wife.

Unquestionably Bridger's chief claim to remembrance by posterity rests upon the extraordinary part he bore in the exploration of the West. The common verdict of his many employers, from Robert Campbell down to Captain Raynolds, is that as a guide he was without an equal. He was a born topographer. The whole West was mapped out in his mind as in an exhaustive atlas. Such was his instinctive sense of locality and direction that it used to be said that he could "smell his way" where he could not see it. He was not only a good topographer in the field, but he could reproduce his impressions in sketches. "With a buffalo skin and a piece of charcoal," says Captain Gunnison, "he will map out any portion of this immense region, and delineate mountains, streams, and the circular valleys, called 'holes,' with wonderful accuracy." His ability in and civilized country. He was among the first who went to the this line caused him always to be in demand as guide to exploring parties, and his name is connected with scores of prominent government and private expeditions.

His lifetime measures that period of our history during which the West was changed from a trackless wilderness to a settled mountains, and he lived to see all that had made a life like his possible swept away forever. His name survives in many a feature of our western geography, but in none with greater honor than in this little lake among the mountains that he knew so well; and near the source of that majestic stream with which so much of his eventful life was identified.

Delusion Lake—M : 9—1878—U. S. G. S.—This lake was long supposed to be an arm of the Yellowstone Lake, and, in the fanciful comparison of the main lake to the form of the human hand, occupied the position of the index finger. The delusion consisted in this mistaken notion of a permanent connection between the two lakes.

173

Gallatin Lake—E : 4—1885—U.S.G.S.—Source of the Gallatin River.

Hart Lake—P:9—According to Hayden, "long known to the hunters of the region as Heart Lake." Named prior to 1870 for an old hunter by the name of Hart Hunney who in early times plied his trade in this vicinity. He was possibly one of Bonneville's men, for he seems to have known the General well and to have been familiar with his operations. He was killed by a war party of Crows in 1852.

The spelling, *Heart,* dates from the expeditions of 1871. The notion that the name arose from the shape of the lake seems to have originated with Captain Barlow. It has generally been accepted although there is really no similarity between the form of the lake and that of a heart. Lewis Lake is the only heart-shaped lake in that locality.

Everts named Hart Lake, Bessie Lake, after his daughter.

Henry Lake—A noted lake outside the limits of the Park passed by tourists entering the park from the west. It is named for a celebrated fur trader, Andrew Henry, who built a trading post in that vicinity in 1809.

Hering Lake—R:5—1878—U.S.G.S.—For Rudolph Hering, Topographer on the Snake River Division of the Hayden Survey for 1872.

Indian Pond—J : 11—1880—Norris—An ancient, much-used camping-ground of Indians. "My favorite camp on the Yellowstone Lake (and it evidently has been a favorite one for the Indian) has ever been upon the grove-dotted bluff, elevated thirty or forty feet above the lake, directly fronting Indian Pond."—Norris.

Isa Lake—L:6—1893—N.P.R.R.—For Miss Isabel Jelke, of Cincinnati.

Jackson Lake—U–W : 6—Date unknown.—For David Jackson, a noted mountaineer and fur trader and one of the first three partners of the Rocky Mountain Fur Company. This lake was discovered by John Colter and was named by Clark *Lake Biddle,* in honor of Nicholas Biddle, who first gave to the world an authentic edition of the journal of the celebrated Lewis and Clark Expedition

Jenny Lake—South of Leigh Lake and off the map.—1872 —U.S.G.S.—For the wife of Richard Leigh. She was a Shoshone Indian.

Leigh Lake—W:5—1872—U.S.G.S.—For Richard Leigh ("Beaver Dick"), a noted hunter, trapper, and guide in the country around the Teton Mountains. The nickname "Beaver Dick" arose, not from the fact that Leigh was an expert beaver trapper, but on account of the striking resemblance of two abnormally large front teeth in his upper jaw to the teeth of a beaver. The Indians called him "The Beaver."

Lewis Lake—O:7—1872—U.S.G.S.—For Captain Lewis of "Lewis and Clark" fame.

"As it had no name, so far as we could ascertain, we decided to call it Lewis Lake, in memory of that gallant explorer Captain Meriwether Lewis. The south fork of the Columbia, which was to have perpetuated his name, has reverted to its Indian title Shoshone, and is commonly known by that name, or its translation, Snake River. As this lake lies near the head of one of the principal forks of that stream, it may not be inappropriately called Lewis Lake."—Bradley.*

Lost Lake—M:7—1885—U.S.G.S.—Characteristic.— This is probably Norris' Two-Ocean Pond, and is doubtless also the lake referred to by Hayden in the following paragraph from his report for 1871:

"We camped at night on the shore of a lake which seemed to have no outlet. It is simply a depression which receives the drainage of the surrounding hills. It is marshy around the shores, and the surface is covered thickly with the leaves and flowers of a large yellow lily."—Hayden.

Madison Lake—N:4—1872—U.S.G.S.—Head of the Madison River.

"A small lake, covering perhaps sixty acres, occupies the southern end of the [Firehole] valley, where it bends to the

* F. V. Hayden, *Sixth Annual Report,* 249.

eastward; and as the ultimate lake source of the Madison River, is the only proper possessor of the name 'Madison Lake.' "— Bradley.*

Mary Lake—J : 7—1873—Tourist Party.—Circumstance recorded by Rev. E. J. Stanley, one of the party, and author of the book *Rambles in Wonderland,* describing the tour. The following extract is from his book:

"We passed along the bank of a lovely little lakelet, sleeping in seclusion in the shade of towering evergreens, by which it is sheltered from the roaring tempests. It is near the divide, and on its pebbly shore some members of our party unfurled the Stars and Stripes, and christened it Mary's Lake, in honor of Miss Clark, a young lady belonging to our party."

This lake appears on Jones's map for the same year as Summit Lake. Everts is said to have passed it in his wanderings, but there is no reliable evidence to that effect.

Riddle Lake—N:8—1872—U.S.G.S.—" 'Lake Riddle' is a fugitive name, which has been located at several places, but nowhere permanently. It is supposed to have been used originally to designate the mythical lake, among the mountains, whence, according to the hunters, water flowed to both oceans. I have agreed to Mr. Hering's proposal to attach the name to this lake, which is directly upon the divide at a point where the waters of the two oceans start so nearly together, and thus to solve the unsolved 'riddle' of the 'two-ocean-water.' "— Bradley.† This was a year before Captain Jones verified the existence of Two-Ocean Pass.

Shoshone Lake—M-N:5–6—1872—U.S.G.S.—From Shoshone, or Snake River, which here finds its source. This lake was first named De Lacy Lake, after its discoverer. The Washburn Party (1870) appear to have named it after their leader. In 1871, Doctor Hayden, failing to identify its location and believing it to be tributary to the Madison River, renamed it Madison Lake. It is this name which appears on the first map of the Park and in the Act of Dedication, where the west boun-

* *Ibid.,* 243.
† *Ibid.,* 250.

dary of the Park is described as being "fifteen miles west of the most western point of Madison Lake." In 1872, when the correct drainage of the lake was discovered, the name "Madison Lake" was transferred to its present location (See *Madison Lake*), and its place supplied by "Shoshone Lake." The Act of Dedication is therefore misleading, and it is necessary to know that "Madison Lake" of the Act, is "Shoshone Lake" now, in order to understand the true location of the west boundary of the Park.

In changing the name from "De Lacy" to "Shoshone," Prof. F. H. Bradley, of the United States Geological Survey, took occasion to reflect severely and unjustifiably upon De Lacy's work in mapping the country.*

De Lacy felt deeply wronged by this action, and Dr. Hayden promised him that he would set the matter right; but nothing was done. At a later day, Colonel Norris endeavored to do De Lacy tardy justice by placing his name on the stream which enters the lake from the north and drains the beautiful valley now crossed by the tourist route. This name remained for several years, when it also was removed by the United States Geological Survey, and its place filled by "Heron Creek." During the past year, however, the name "De Lacy Creek" has been restored.

Yellowstone Lake—K-O : 8–12—From the river which flows through it. This lake was named, on the map showing "Colter's Route in 1807," Lake Eustis, in honor of William Eustis, Secretary of War to President Madison, 1809 to 1812.

Later it appears as Sublette Lake, in honor of the noted fur trader, William Sublette. It is even said at one time to have borne the "fugitive name," Riddle Lake. But it early became known by its present name.

The islands of this lake are seven in number. They seem to have all been named by the United States Geological Survey largely for the employes of the survey. They are:

Carrington Island—For Campbell Carrington, zoologist.

* *Ibid.,* 244.

177

Dot Island—A mere dot on the map.

Frank Island—For the brother of Henry W. Elliott, a member of the Hayden Expedition of 1871. This Island was renamed Belknap Island in 1875 by the members of Secretary Belknap's party, who passed through the Park in that year. The name, however, never came into use.

Molly Island—For the wife of Mr. Henry Gannett.

Peale Island—For Dr. A. C. Peale, author of the elaborate report on thermal springs which appears in Hayden's report for 1878.

Pelican Roost—Characteristic.

Stevenson Island—For James Stevenson. See *Mt. Stevenson*.

The bays are also seven in number, of which only the following merit notice:

Mary Bay—Named by Henry W. Elliott for Miss Mary Force.

Thumb—From the old fancy that the form of the lake resembled that of the human hand.

Bridge Bay—From Bridge Creek. See *Bridge Creek*.

The capes are thirteen in number. We need notice only Signal Point, which was much used in signaling by the early explorers; Steamboat Point, named from the Steamboat Springs near by; and Storm Point, so named because it receives the full force of the prevailing south-west winds from across the lake.

"The Annie."—The first boat on the Yellowstone Lake was a small canvas craft 12 feet long by 3½ feet wide. Dr. Hayden records that it was christened *The Annie,* "by Mr. Stevenson, in compliment to Miss Anna L. Dawes, the amiable daughter of Hon. H. L. Dawes."

The boat was extemporized by Mr. James Stevenson from such materials as could be picked up. In the classic picture of this historic craft, the persons in the boat are James Stevenson and Henry W. Elliott.

VI

Miscellaneous Features

Craig Pass—L:6—1891—From the maiden name of Mrs. Ida Craig Wilcox, the first tourist to cross the pass.

Hayden Valley—H-J: 8–10—1878—U.S.G.S.—For the eminent American geologist, Ferdinand Vandiveer Hayden, M.D., LL.D., whose important part in the history of the Yellowstone National Park has been fully set forth in previous pages. The following condensed sketch of his life is from the pen of Dr. A. C. Peale:*

" . . . He was born at Westfield, Mass., September 7, 1829. . . . His father died when he was about ten years of age, and about two years later he went to live with an uncle at Rochester, in Lorain County, Ohio, where he remained for six years. He taught in the country district schools of the neighborhood during his sixteenth and seventeenth years, and at the age of eighteen went to Oberlin College, where he was graduated in 1850. . . .

"He studied medicine with Dr. J. S. Newberry, at Cleveland, and at Albany was graduated Doctor of Medicine in the early part of 1853. After his graduation, he was sent by Prof. James Hall, of New York, to the Bad Lands of White River, in Dakota. The years 1854 and 1855 he spent exploring and collecting fossils in the Upper Missouri country, mainly at his own expense. From 1856 until 1859, he was connected as geologist with the expeditions of Lieutenant Warren, engaged in explorations in Nebraska and Dakota. From 1859 until 1862, he was surgeon, naturalist, and geologist with Captain W. F. Raynolds,

* Philosophical Society of Washington, *Bulletin,* Vol. XI (1892), 476–78.

in the exploration of the Yellowstone and Missouri Rivers. In October, 1862, he was appointed acting assistant surgeon and assistant medical inspector until June, 1865, when he resigned, and was brevetted lieutenant-colonel for meritorious services during the war. He then resumed his scientific work, and in 1866 made another trip to the Bad Lands of Dakota, this time in the interest of the Academy of Natural Sciences of Philadelphia. In 1865, he was elected professor of mineralogy and geology in the University of Pennsylvania, which position he resigned in 1872. From 1867 to 1879, his history is that of the organization of which he had charge, which began as a geological survey of Nebraska, and became finally the Geological Survey of the Territories. . . . From 1879 until December, 1886, he was connected with the United States Geological Survey as geologist. His health began to fail soon after his connection with this organization, and gradually became worse, and he lived only a year after his resignation.

"In 1876, the degree of LL.D. was conferred upon him by the University of Rochester, and in June, 1886, he received the same degree from the University of Pennsylvania. He was a member of seventeen scientific societies in the United States, among them the National Academy of Sciences, and was honorary and corresponding member of some seventy foreign societies. A bibliography of his writings includes 158 titles.

" . . . The gentleness and diffidence, approaching even timidity, which impressed his fellow-students at Oberlin, characterized Dr. Hayden throughout his life, and rendered it somewhat difficult for those who did not know him intimately to understand the reasons for his success, which was undoubtedly due to his energy and perseverance, qualities which were equally characteristic of him as a boy and student and in later life. His desire to forward the cause of science was sincere and enthusiastic, and he was always ready to modify his views upon the presentation of evidence. He was intensely nervous, frequently impulsive, but ever generous, and his honesty and integrity undoubted. The greater part of his work for the government and for science was a labor of love."

Jones Pass—K : 12—1880—Norris—For its discoverer, Captain W. A. Jones, Corps of Engineers, U.S.A., who passed through it in 1873.

Kingman Pass—D : 6—1883—U.S.G.S.—The pass of which Golden Gate is the northern entrance. For Lieutenant D. C. Kingman, Corps of Engineers, U.S.A., who built the road through the pass.

Norris Geyser Basin—G-H:6—For P. W. Norris, who first explored and described it, and opened it up to tourists. It was, however, discovered in 1872 by E. S. Topping and Dwight Woodruff, who were led in that direction by noticing from the summit of Bunsen Peak a vast column of steam ascending to the southward. The day after this discovery, a tourist party, including a Mr. and Mrs. H. H. Stone, of Bozeman, Montana, visited it from Mammoth Hot Springs, and then continued their course, by way of the general line of the present route, to the Firehole Geyser Basin. Mrs. Stone was the first white woman to visit the Park.

Norris Pass—M:6—1879—Norris—For its discoverer.

Raynolds Pass—Not on map.—Crosses the Continental Divide to the northward of Henry Lake and connects the valley of Henry Fork with that of the Madison. Named for Captain W. F. Raynolds, who led his expedition through it in 1860.

Targhee Pass—Not on map.—Crosses the Continental Divide to the eastward of Henry Lake and leads from the valley of Henry Fork to that of the Madison. The origin and orthography of this name are uncertain. In Hayden's Report for 1872, occur three spellings, Targhee, Tyghee, and Tahgee. The weight of evidence is in favor of the form here adopted. There was an impression among the Hayden Survey people, in 1872, that the name was given in honor of some distinguished Indian Chief; but that there was no definite information on the point is evident from the following statements, taken from Hayden's Report for 1872. On page 56, it is stated that *Tahgee Pass* "was named years ago for the head chief of the Bannocks." On page 227, it is said that *Tyghee* Pass "was named for an old Shoshone chief who was wont to use it." The real origin is thus

181

left somewhat obscure, but it is probable that the notion that the pass was named for an Indian chief may have some foundation in fact. There was living among the Bannocks within the present memory of white men a chief whose name was pronounced *Ti-gee*.

LEGISLATION AFFECTING THE YELLOWSTONE NATIONAL PARK

The Act of Dedication

AN ACT to set apart a certain tract of land lying near the headwaters of the Yellowstone River as a public park.

Be it enacted by the Senate and House of Representatives of the United States of America in Congress assembled, That the tract of land in the Territories of Montana and Wyoming lying near the headwaters of the Yellowstone River, and described as follows, to wit: commencing at the junction of Gardiner's River with the Yellowstone River and running east of the meridian, passing ten miles to the eastward of the most eastern point of Yellowstone Lake; thence south along the said meridian to the parallel of latitude, passing ten miles south of the most southern point of Yellowstone Lake; thence west along said parallel to the meridian, passing fifteen miles west of the most western point of Madison Lake; thence north along said meridian to the latitude of the junction of the Yellowstone and Gardiner's Rivers; thence east to the place of beginning, is hereby reserved and withdrawn from settlement, occupancy, or sale under the laws of the United States, and dedicated and set apart as a public park or pleasuring ground for the benefit and enjoyment of the people; and all persons who shall locate, or settle upon, or occupy the same or any part thereof, except as hereinafter provided, shall be considered trespassers and removed therefrom.

Sec. 2. That said public park shall be under the exclusive control of the Secretary of the Interior, whose duty it shall be as soon as practicable, to make and publish such rules and regulations as he may deem necessary or proper for the care and management of the same. Such regulations shall provide for the preservation from injury or spoliation of all timber, mineral deposits, natural curiosities, or wonders within said park, and their retention in their natural condition.

The Secretary may, in his discretion, grant leases for building purposes, for terms not exceeding ten years, of small parcels of ground, at such places in said park as shall require the erection of buildings for the accommodation of visitors; all of the proceeds of said leases, and other revenues that may be derived from any source connected with said park, to be expended under his direction in the management of the same and the construction of roads and bridle-paths therein. He shall provide against the wanton destruction of the fish and game found within said park and against their capture or destruction for the purposes of merchandise or profit. He shall also cause all persons trespassing upon the same after the passage of this act to be removed therefrom, and generally shall be authorized to take all such measures as shall be necessary or proper to fully carry out the objects and purposes of this act.

Approved March 1, 1872.

Signed by:

JAMES G. BLAINE, *Speaker of the House*

SCHUYLER COLFAX, *Vice-President of the United States and President of the Senate*

ULYSSES S. GRANT, *President of the United States*

Military Assistance Authorized for Protecting the Park Sundry Civil Bill for 1883

. . . The Secretary of War, upon the request of the Secretary of the Interior, is hereby authorized and directed to make the necessary details of troops to prevent trespassers or intruders from entering the park for the purpose of destroying the game or objects of curiosity therein, or for any other purpose prohibited by law, and to remove such persons from the park if found therein. . . .

Approved, March 3, 1883

Admission of the State of Wyoming

SEC. 2. . . . *Provided,* That nothing in this act contained shall repeal or affect any act of Congress relating to the Yellowstone National Park, or the reservation of the park as now defined, or as may be hereafter defined or extended, or the power of the United States over it; and nothing contained in this act shall interfere with the right and ownership of the United States in said park and reservation as it now is or may hereafter be defined or extended by law: but exclusive legislation, in all cases whatsoever, shall be exercised by the United States, which shall have exclusive control and jurisdiction over the same; but nothing in this proviso contained shall be construed to prevent the service within said park of civil and criminal process lawfully issued by the authority of said state; and the said state shall not be entitled to select indemnity school lands for the sixteenth and thirty-sixth sections that may be in said park reservation, as the same is now defined or may be hereafter defined. . . .

Approved, July 10, 1890.

The National Park Protective Act

AN ACT to protect the birds and animals in Yellowstone National Park, and to punish crimes in said park, and for other purposes.

Be it enacted by the Senate and House of Representatives of the United States of America in Congress assembled, That the Yellowstone National Park, as its boundaries now are defined, or as they may be hereafter defined or extended, shall be under the sole and exclusive jurisdiction of the United States; and that all the laws applicable to places under the sole and exclusive jurisdiction of the United States shall have force and effect in said park; provided, however, that nothing in this Act shall be construed to forbid the service in the park of any civil or criminal process of any court having jurisdiction in the States of Idaho, Montana, and Wyoming. All fugitives from justice taking refuge in said park shall be subject to the

185

same laws as refugees from justice found in the State of Wyoming.

SEC. 2. That said park, for all the purposes of this Act, shall constitute a part of the United States judicial district of Wyoming and the District and Circuit Courts of the United States in and for said district shall have jurisdiction of all offenses committed within said park.

SEC. 3. That if any offense shall be committed in said Yellowstone National Park, which offense is not prohibited or the punishment is not specially provided for by any law of the United States or by any regulation of the Secretary of the Interior, the offender shall be subject to the same punishment as the laws of the State of Wyoming in force at the time of the commission of the offense may provide for a like offense in the said State; and no subsequent repeal of any such law of the State of Wyoming shall affect any prosecution for said offense committed within said park.

SEC. 4. That all hunting, or the killing, wounding, or capturing at any time of any bird or wild animal, except dangerous animals, when it is necessary to prevent them from destroying human life or inflicting an injury, is prohibited within the limits of said park; nor shall any fish be taken out of the waters of the park by means of seines, nets, traps, or by the use of drugs or any explosive substances or compounds, or in any other way than by hook and line, and then only at such seasons and in such times and manner as may be directed by the Secretary of the Interior. That the Secretary of the Interior shall make and publish such rules and regulations as he may deem necessary and proper for the management and care of the park and for the protection of the property therein, especially for the preservation from injury or spoliation of all timber, mineral deposits, natural curiosities, or wonderful objects within said park; and for the protection of the animals and birds in the park, from capture or destruction, or to prevent their being frightened or driven from the park; and he shall make rules and regulations governing the taking of fish from the streams or lakes in the park. Possession within the said park of the

186

dead bodies, or any part thereof, of any wild bird or animal shall be prima facie evidence that the person or persons having the same are guilty of violating this Act. Any person or persons, or stage or express company or railway company, receiving for transportation any of the said animals, birds or fish so killed, taken or caught, shall be deemed guilty of a misdemeanor, and shall be fined for every such offense, not exceeding three hundred dollars. Any person found guilty of violating any of the provisions of this Act or any rule or regulation that may be promulgated by the Secretary of the Interior with reference to the management and care of the park, or for the protection of the property therein, for the preservation from injury or spoliation of timber, mineral deposits, natural curiosities or wonderful objects within said park, or for the protection of the animals, birds, and fish in the said park, shall be deemed guilty of a misdemeanor, and shall be subjected to a fine of not more than one thousand dollars or imprisonment not exceeding two years, or both, and be adjudged to pay all costs of the proceedings.

That all guns, traps, teams, horses, or means of transportation of every nature or description used by any person or persons within said park limits when engaged in killing, trapping, ensnaring, or capturing such wild beasts, birds, or wild animals shall be forfeited to the United States, and may be seized by the officers in said park and held pending the prosecution of any person or persons arrested under charge of violating the provisions of this Act, and upon conviction under this Act of such person or persons using said guns, traps, teams, horses, or other means of transportation, such forfeiture shall be adjudicated as a penalty in addition to the other punishment provided in this Act. Such forfeited property shall be disposed and accounted for by and under the authority of the Secretary of the Interior.

SEC. 5. That the United States Circuit Court in said district shall appoint a commissioner, who shall reside in the park, who shall have jurisdiction to hear and act upon all complaints made, of any and all violations of the law, or of the rules and regulations made by the Secretary of the Interior for the government of the park, and for the protection of the animals, birds, and fish and objects of interest therein, and for other purposes authorized by this Act. Such commissioner shall have power, upon sworn information, to issue process in the name of the United States for the arrest of any person charged with the commission of any misdemeanor, or charged with the violation of the rules and regulations, or with the violation of any provision of this Act prescribed for the government of said park, and for the protection of the animals, birds, and fish in the said park, and to try the person so charged, and, if found guilty, to impose the punishment and adjudge the forfeiture prescribed. In all cases of conviction, an appeal shall lie from the judgment of said commissioner to the United States District Court for the district of Wyoming, said appeal to be governed by the laws of the State of Wyoming providing for appeals in cases of misdemeanor from justices of the peace to the District Court of said State; but the United States Circuit Court in said district may prescribe rules of procedure and practice for said commissioner in the trial of cases, and for appeal to said United States District Court. Said commissioner shall also have power to issue process as hereinbefore provided for the arrest of any person charged with the commission of any felony within the park, and to summarily hear the evidence introduced, and, if he shall determine that probable cause is shown for holding the person so charged for trial, shall cause such person to be safely conveyed to a secure place for confinement, within the jurisdiction of the United States District Court in said State of Wyoming, and shall certify a transcript of the record of his proceedings and the testimony in the case to the said court, which court shall have jurisdiction of the case; provided, that the said commissioner shall grant bail in all cases bailable under the laws of the United States or of said State. All process issued by the commissioner shall be directed to the marshal of the United States for the district of Wyoming; but nothing herein contained shall be construed

188

as preventing the arrest by any officer of the government or employe of the United States in the park, without process, of any person taken in the act of violating the law or any regulation of the Secretary of the Interior; provided, that the said commissioner shall only exercise such authority and powers as are conferred by this Act.

SEC. 6. That the marshal of the United States for the district of Wyoming may appoint one or more deputy marshals for said park, who shall reside in said park, and the said United States District and Circuit Courts shall hold one session of said courts annually at the town of Sheridan, in the State of Wyoming, and may also hold other sessions at any other place in said State of Wyoming, or in said National Park, at such dates as the said courts may order.

SEC. 7. That the commissioner provided for in this Act shall, in addition to the fees allowed by law to commissioners of the Circuit Courts of the United States, be paid an annual salary of one thousand dollars, payable quarterly, and the marshal of the United States, and his deputies, and the attorney of the United States and his assistants in said district, shall be paid the same compensation and fees as are now provided by law for like services in said district.

SEC. 8. That all costs and expenses arising in cases under this Act, and properly chargeable to the United States, shall be certified, approved, and paid as like costs and expenses in the courts of the United States are certified, approved, and paid under the laws of the United States.

SEC. 9. That the Secretary of the Interior shall cause to be erected in the park a suitable building to be used as a jail, and also having in said building an office for the use of the commissioner, the cost of such building not to exceed five thousand dollars, to be paid out of any moneys in the Treasury not otherwise appropriated, upon the certificate of the Secretary as a voucher therefor.

SEC. 10. That this Act shall not be construed to repeal existing laws conferring upon the Secretary of the Interior and the

189

Secretary of War certain powers with reference to the protection, improvement, and control of the said Yellowstone National Park.

Approved, May 7, 1894

Leases in the Yellowstone National Park

AN ACT concerning leases in the Yellowstone National Park.

Be it enacted by the Senate and House of Representatives of the United States of America in Congress assembled, That the Secretary of the Interior is hereby authorized and empowered to lease to any person, corporation, or company, for a period not exceeding ten years, at such annual rental as the Secretary of the Interior may determine, parcels of land in the Yellowstone National Park, of not more than ten acres in extent for each tract, and not in excess of twenty acres in all to any one person, corporation, or company, on which may be erected hotels and necessary out-buildings; provided, that such lease or leases shall not include any of the geysers or other objects of curiosity or interest in said park, or exclude the public from free and convenient approach thereto, or include any ground within one-eighth of a mile of any of the geysers or the Yellowstone Falls, the Grand Cañon, or the Yellowstone River, Mammoth Hot Springs, or any object of curiosity in the park; and provided, further, that such leases shall not convey, either expressly or by implication, any exclusive privilege within the park except upon the premises held thereunder and for the time therein granted. Every lease hereafter made for any property in said park shall require the lessee to observe and obey each and every provision in any Act of Congress, and every rule, order, or regulation made, or which may hereafter be made and published by the Secretary of the Interior concerning the use, care, management, or government of the park, or any object or property therein, under penalty of forfeiture of such lease, and every such lease shall be subject to the right of revocation and forfeiture, which shall therein be reserved by the

190

Secretary of the Interior; and provided, further, that persons or corporations now holding leases of ground in the park may, upon the surrender thereof, be granted new leases hereunder, and upon the terms and stipulations contained in their present leases, with such modifications, restrictions, and reservations as the Secretary of the Interior may prescribe.

This Act, however, is not to be construed as mandatory upon the Secretary of the Interior, but the authority herein given is to be exercised in his sound discretion.

That so much of that portion of the Act of March third, eighteen hundred and eighty-three, relating to the Yellowstone Park, as conflicts with this Act, be, and the same is hereby, repealed.

Approved, August 3, 1894.

APPROPRIATIONS FOR THE YELLOWSTONE NATIONAL PARK

Act June 20, 1878	To protect, preserve, and improve the Park	$10,000.00
Mar. 3, 1879	To protect, preserve, and improve the Park	10,000.00
June 16, 1880	To protect, preserve, and improve the Park	15,000.00
Mar. 3, 1881	To protect, preserve, and improve the Park	15,000.00
Mar. 3, 1881	Deficiency for 1880	89.76
Aug. 5, 1882	Deficiency for 1881	155.00
Aug. 7, 1882	For protection and improvement of Park	15,000.00
Aug. 7, 1882	To reimburse P. W. Norris for salary and expenses, April 18, 1877, to June 30, 1878	3,180.41
Mar. 3, 1883	For protection and improvement of Park	40,000.00
July 7, 1884	For protection and improvement of Park	40,000.00
Mar. 3, 1885	For protection and improvement of Park	40,000.00
Joint Resolution of July 1 and July 15, 1886	Compensation of Superintendent and employes for month of July, 1886	934.25
Act Aug. 4, 1886	For construction of roads and bridges	20,000.00

Mar.	3, 1887	For construction of roads and bridges	20,000.00
Oct.	2, 1888	For construction of roads and bridges	25,000.00
Mar.	2, 1889	For construction of roads and bridges	50,000.00
Aug.	30, 1890	For construction of roads and bridges	75,000.00
Sept.	30, 1890	Reimbursement of Super-intendent Conger	169.37
Mar.	3, 1891	For construction of roads and bridges	75,000.00
Aug.	5, 1892	For construction of roads and bridges	45,000.00
Mar.	3, 1893	For construction of roads and bridges	30,000.00
May	4, 1894	For erection of court-house and jail	5,000.00
Aug.	18, 1894	For construction of roads and bridges	30,000.00
Aug.	18, 1894	For salary of Commission-er provided by Act of May 4, 1894	1,000.00
Mar.	2, 1895	For construction of roads and bridges	30,000.00
Mar.	2, 1895	For salary of Commissioner	1,000.00
Mar.	2, 1895	For reimbursement of John W. Meldrum	385.75
		Total	$596,914.54

Receipts from leases	$8,358.94	
Expenditures from same	4,053.45	
Balance		4,305.49
Outlay for 23 years		$592,609.05
Average annual outlay less than		25,000.00

LIST OF SUPERINTENDENTS OF THE
YELLOWSTONE NATIONAL PARK

Name	Length of Service	Compensation
Nathaniel P. Langford	Appointed May 10, 1872; removed April 18, 1877	No compensation
Philetus W. Norris	Appointed April 18, 1877	No compensation
	Commissioned July 5, 1878; removed February 2, 1882	$1,500 per annum
Patrick H. Conger	Commissioned February 2, 1882; resigned July 28, 1884	$2,000 per annum
Robert E. Carpenter	Commissioned August 4, 1884; removed May 29, 1885	$2,000 per annum
David W. Wear	Commissioned May 29, 1885. Congress failed to appropriate for office from August 1, 1886	$2,000 per annum
Capt. Moses Harris	Acting Superintendent of Park. August 10, 1886, detailed by Secretary	

	of War, in pursuance of Act March 3, 1883 (22 Statutes, 627). Relieved from duty June 1, 1889	No compensation other than army pay
Capt. F. A. Boutelle	Acting Superintendent of Park; assigned June 1, 1889, relieving Capt. Moses Harris	No compensation other than army pay
Capt. George S. Anderson	Acting Superintendent of Park; assigned January 21, 1891, relieving Capt. F. A. Boutelle	No compensation other than army pay

195

BIBLIOGRAPHY

Secondary Works of Interest to the General Reader

Alter, J. Cecil. *Jim Bridger*. Norman, University of Oklahoma Press, 1962.

Augspurger, Marie M. *Yellowstone National Park: Historical and Descriptive*. Middletown, Ohio, published by the author, 1948.

Bakeless, John. *Lewis and Clark, Partners in Discovery*. New York, Morrow and Co., 1947.

Bancroft, Hubert Howe. *History of Washington, Montana, and Idaho*. San Francisco, The History Co., 1896.

Bartlett, Richard A. *Great Surveys of the American West*. Norman, University of Oklahoma Press, 1962.

Beal, Merrill D. *The Story of Man in Yellowstone*. Revised edition. Yellowstone Park, Wyoming. The Yellowstone Library and Museum Association, 1960.

————. *"I Will Fight No More Forever": Chief Joseph and the Nez Perce War*. Seattle, University of Washington Press, 1963.

Bonney, Orrin H., and Lorraine Bonney. *Guide to the Wyoming Mountains and Wilderness Areas*. Denver, Sage Books, 1960.

Burlingame, Merrill G. *The Montana Frontier*. Helena, State Publishing Co., 1942.

Carpenter, Frank D., *Adventures in Geyser Land*. Ed. by Heister Dean Guie and Lucullus Virgil McWhorter. Caldwell, Idaho, The Caxton Printers, Inc., 1935.

196

Catlin, George. *North American Indians*. 2 vols. Edinburgh, John Grant, 1926.

Chittenden, Hiram Martin. *The American Fur Trade of the Far West*. 2 vols. New York, Press of the Pioneers, 1935.

———, and Alfred T. Richardson. *Life, Letters, and Travels of Father Pierre-Jean De Smet, S. J., 1801–1873*. 4 vols. New York, F. P. Harper, 1904–1905.

Coues, Elliott. *The History of the Expedition Under the Command of Lewis and Clark*. 4 vols. New York, Francis P. Harper, 1893.

Crampton, Louis C. *Early History of Yellowstone National Park and Its Relations to National Park Policies*. Washington, Government Printing Office, 1923.

Dale, H. C. *The Ashley-Smith Explorations*. Cincinnati, The Arthur H. Clark Co., 1918.

De Voto, Bernard. *Across the Wide Missouri*. Boston, Houghton Mifflin Co., 1947.

———. *The Journals of Lewis and Clark*. Boston, Houghton Mifflin Co., 1953.

Dunraven, the Earl of. *Hunting in the Yellowstone*. New York, The Macmillan Co., 1925.

Ewers, John C. *The Blackfeet: Raiders of the Northwestern Plains*. Norman, University of Oklahoma Press, 1958.

Ferris, Warren A. *Life in the Rocky Mountains, 1830–35*. Ed. by Paul Chrisler Phillips. Denver, Old West Publishing Co. (Fred Rosenstock), 1940.

Gard, Wayne. *The Great Buffalo Hunt*. New York, Alfred Knopf, 1959.

Goetzmann, William H. *Army Exploration in the American West, 1803–1863*. New Haven, Yale University Press, 1959.

Goodwin, Cardinal. *The Trans-Mississippi West (1803–1853)*. New York, D. Appleton and Co., 1922.

Gray, Arthur Amos. *Men Who Built the West*. Caldwell, Idaho, The Caxton Printers, 1945.

Hafen, LeRoy, and Ann W. Hafen, eds. *The Diaries of William Henry Jackson*. Vol. X in The Far West and the Rockies Historical Series. Glendale, The Arthur H. Clark Co., 1959.

197

Haines, Francis. *The Nez Percés: Tribesmen of the Columbia Plateau*. Norman, University of Oklahoma Press, 1955.

Harris, Burton. *John Colter: His Years in the Rockies*. New York, Charles Scribner's Sons, 1952.

Haynes, Jack E. *Haynes Guide to Yellowstone*. Various editions. St. Paul, Haynes, Inc.

Irving, Washington. *The Adventures of Captain Bonneville, U.S.A.* Ed. by Edgeley W. Todd. Norman, University of Oklahoma Press, 1961.

Jackson, Willian H. *Time Exposure*. New York, G. P. Putnam's Sons, 1940.

Langford, Nathaniel Pitt. *The Discovery of Yellowstone Park, 1870*. St. Paul, J. E. Haynes, 1923.

Lowie, Robert H. *The Crow Indians*. New York, Farrar and Rinehart, 1935.

Mattes, Merrill J. *Behind the Legend of Colter's Hell: The Early History of Yellowstone National Park*. Reprinted from the *Mississippi Valley Historical Review,* Vol. XXXVI, No. 2 (September, 1949) and distributed by the Wyoming State Historical Society.

Phillips, Paul Chrisler. *The Fur Trade*. 2 vols. Norman, University of Oklahoma Press, 1961.

Quaife, Milo M., ed. *"Yellowstone Kelly": The Memoirs of Luther S. Kelly*. New Haven, Yale University Press, 1926.

Randell, Leslie W. (Gay). *Footprints Along the Yellowstone*. San Antonio, The Naylor Co., 1961.

Ross, Alexander. *The Fur Hunters of the Far West*. Ed. by Kenneth A. Spalding. University of Oklahoma Press, 1956.

Sandoz, Mari. *The Buffalo Hunters*. New York, Hastings House, 1954.

Schultz, James Willard. *Blackfeet and Buffalo*. Ed. by Keith C. Seele. Norman, University of Oklahoma Press, 1962.

Sunder, John E. *Bill Sublette, Mountain Man*. Norman, University of Oklahoma Press, 1959.

Thwaites, Reuben Gold, ed. *Early Western Travels*. 32 vols. Cincinnati, The Arthur H. Clark Co., 1905.

Toole, K. Ross. *Montana: An Uncommon Land*. Norman, University of Oklahoma Press, 1959.

Topping, E. S. *The Chronicles of the Yellowstone*. St. Paul, Pioneer Press Co., 1888.

Victor, Francis Fuller. *The River of the West*. Hartford, R. W. Bliss and Co., 1870.

Vinton, Stallo. *John Colter, Discoverer of Yellowstone Park*. New York, Edward Eberstadt, 1926.

Wheat, Carl I. *Mapping the Trans-Mississippi West, 1540–1861*. 5 vols. San Francisco, The Institute of Historical Cartography, 1957–63.

Writers Program, W.P.A. *Idaho: A Guide in Word and Pictures*. Caldwell, The Caxton Printers, 1937.

———. *Montana: A State Guide Book*. New York, Viking Press, 1939.

———. *Wyoming: A Guide to Its History, Highways, and People*. New York, Oxford University Press, 1941.

INDEX

Names in the appendices are not included in this index.